D1478245

Love

First

A Children's Ministry for the Whole Church

COLETTE POTTS

CHURCH
PUBLISHING
INCORPORATED

Copyright © 2018 by Colette Potts

All rights reserved. No part of this book may be reproduced, stored in a retrieval system, or transmitted in any form or by any means, electronic or mechanical, including photocopying, recording, or otherwise, without the written permission of the publisher.

Unless otherwise noted, the Scripture quotations contained herein are from the New Revised Standard Version Bible, copyright © 1989 by the Division of Christian Education of the National Council of Churches of Christ in the U.S.A. Used by permission. All rights reserved.

Church Publishing
19 East 34th Street
New York, NY 10016
www.churchpublishing.org

Cover design and typesetting by Beth Oberholtzer

Library of Congress Cataloging-in-Publication Data

Names: Potts, Colette, author.
Title: Love first : a children's ministry for the whole church / Colette Potts.
Description: New York : Church Publishing, 2018. | Includes bibliographical references.
Identifiers: LCCN 2018010536 (print) | LCCN 2018027047 (ebook) | ISBN
    9781640650657 (ebook) | ISBN 9781640650640 (pbk.)
Subjects: LCSH: Church work with children.
Classification: LCC BV639.C4 (ebook) | LCC BV639.C4 P68 2018 (print) | DDC
    259/.22—dc23
LC record available at https://lccn.loc.gov/2018010536

Printed in the United States of America

For Millie, Sammy and Danny:
Three reasons I need
the world to be more loving

Contents

Foreword   vii

Acknowledgments   xi

Preface   xiii

Introduction   xvii

CHAPTER 1: Our Challenges   1

CHAPTER 2: Our Leap   9

CHAPTER 3: Our Sacred Spaces   16

CHAPTER 4: Our Precious Hour   31

CHAPTER 5: Our Curriculum   44

CHAPTER 6: Our Gifts   59

CHAPTER 7: Our Ministers   78

CHAPTER 8: Our Worship   92

Epilogue   107

APPENDIX A: Heartbeats   109

APPENDIX B: Suggested Bible Stories   120

APPENDIX C: Recommended Book List   127

Foreword

"This is the story *of our mid-size Episcopal church's struggle to reach today's young families. The process of self-reflection helped us locate the intersection of the needs of children, families, and the church. We took a risk to rethink (completely) how we teach children about God, religion, faith, and the church in a way that is meaningful to children, families, and our faith community today—and in the future. We erased our pre-conceived notions about what we thought we needed, we recycled the old curricula, emptied the rooms, and moved forward with one single commitment: make it all meaningful. What resulted was a program that the whole church was proud of, one that children and parents loved and teachers wanted to teach, and a new way of being that breathed life into our congregation. We finally had what we really needed. And we did it ourselves." (page xix)*

When I was serving as the Missioner for Education, Formation, and Discipleship in the Episcopal Diocese of Massachusetts, I started to hear about a new program at a church on Cape Cod. At first it was the rector telling me that they were trying some exciting new things in the children's program. Many months later the interim called me to let me know that there was something really different and energizing happening with their Sunday school. And now Colette Potts is sharing their story and strategy with the world.

In the sea of religious formation books, this book stands out for me because it is a framework, not a curriculum. Colette calls it "an approach to living in community." This is the story of St. Barnabas's Episcopal Church changing how children are invited into the life of the community and centering on the value of loving God and loving neighbor. In one sense, it is so simple. But in another sense, this type of change requires listening to the needs and desires of busy families, being willing to clean everything out and start over, and simplifying and grounding the message of a church school program. Colette Potts is a family therapist and takes an authentically different approach to the issues that a lot of churches face: declining attendance, unengaged children, and parents who want help with parenting. She provides a way into the heart of the issue that I haven't encountered before.

Her approach is deceptively simple—putting love first. But the practice is sometimes counter to our institutional trappings and tradition. The church spends a lot of time teaching *about* love, rather than having children and adults actually practice it together. This book calls for changing expectations about the goals of church programs and the values that underlie them in order to help children and adults love one another and the world. Colette takes the reader through her church's process.

Colette started by asking the question "What can the church offer to families that they can't get somewhere else?" Recent research shows that parents want their kids to be good, kind, loving people but are having a hard time teaching that in today's culture. Church seems like a natural place for parents to get help for this. So how can the church help children be more loving, kind, and empathetic? Empathy alone is not the end of the message, but when the church teaches children empathy and how to love self and one's neighbor, then religion is not just language disconnected from everyday life. One reason for folks' leaving organized religion is that they feel the church is hypocritical. This approach helps the church do a better job of connecting talk of faith into action in the world in an authentic, community-centered way.

This book dives deep into the process of change, critically examining the space, the limits of time, the formation possibilities in liturgy, and the gifts embedded within the community itself. Colette describes the rhythm of their revamped Sunday morning program as well as the thought process behind each of their choices, not as a program to copy but as a guideline for understanding the essential elements to create a meaningful program in any context. It's not about all the activities—the activities are the outcome of thinking deeply and critically about all the aspects in church that connect formation to anyone entering the doors. There are lots of practical suggestions as well as different ways of looking at the things that churches always do. Rather than a "how-to," though, this book encourages rethinking church in your own context.

What are the challenges for your congregation? Are you wondering why you don't have young families? Colette offers an approach to change—a realistic evaluation of your program and your congregation—rooted in the outlook, goals, and desires of the congregation. This is about church helping kids have a faith life that grows with them and helps them to apply faith to real world situations in a way that anticipates an adult faith in the church.

Are you having trouble getting teachers? There are wonderful insights and stories to help you rethink and reshape teacher recruitment. Colette shares the belief that it isn't about finding the perfect teacher, or the knowledgeable Bible scholar that will involve more adults in teaching. Her approach is connecting the gifts of the adults in the congregation with the children, which has led to multiplying the numbers of adults who teach, lead, mentor, and share with the children and youth of St. Barnabas.

Do your children's spaces need some TLC after years of neglect? Is your church welcoming to children and their parents? Looking realistically at church spaces is part of the process. Every church has both positives and negatives when it comes to space. This book lays out a framework for creating inviting, family-friendly space and considers it as much of the message as any words spoken. This process also suggests ways to create rooms that are set up for spiritual practices—teaching kids ways to think about God and their faith in a meaningful, ritualistic way. These are practices, or spiritual disciplines, that can stay with that child all their life.

This approach honors the fact that many parents were raised with no church, or perhaps bad church experiences. This approach seeks to meet adults where they are as parents in their desire to raise loving, empathetic children and to help them grow in a foundation of love of self, love of neighbor, and love of God. The testimonials from parents that are scattered throughout this book help to emphasize the healing nature of this framework. When too many adults in the church feel inadequate to teach because of their lack of knowledge, and adults outside the church have often been hurt by the church in their own childhood, it is noticeably different to find an approach that takes the Bible seriously as foundation but teaches an embodied, not intellectual, faith.

I commend this book to anyone who is in charge of a children's program at a church, for clergy looking to make meaningful changes in programs, and for parents who are wondering how churches can help in the process of raising loving children.

Amy Cook
Working Group Head for Faith Formation
Episcopal Diocese of California

Acknowledgments

It took the whole church to create the children's ministry at Saint Barnabas: parents and grandparents who brought their children to our classrooms, the unlikely parishioners who volunteered throughout the year, and the generous people who donated to our service projects. If our children's ministry is for the whole church, then so is this book.

This book grew out of a project that could not have happened without the following people: Cyndy Ogden, one of Saint Barnabas's hardest workers and an admired predecessor; Margaret Margolis, my friend and colleague with the best ideas; Louise Forrest, our interim priest, whose kind and generous words made this spread like wildfire; Libby Gibson, for invaluable persistence and wisdom; Patti Barrett, our former rector, who took the first leap of faith and never regretted it; and the diehard Sunday school families (the real reason I took the job).

There is no project, no program, and no book without the talented and dedicated Saint Barnabas Sunday school teachers: Katie Behunin, Jackie Davin, Heather Grey, Bette Hecox, and Flannery Rogers. It was the love and support of these women that made it something special.

And, of course, no work could get done without loving Saint Barnabas friends to care for Millie, Sammy, and Danny when these ideas were coming to bear. Thank you to Maureen Twohig Wormelle, Kathy Wessling, Rachael Rhude, Jennifer Park, and Jessica Fielder for stepping in *before* the going got tough.

Acknowledgments

To all of my parents: Pat and Petur Gudlaugsson, Dan and Deb Sgambati, and Dan and Miyoko Potts—for the good times *and* for those hard times, but most of all for the loving times. I'm grateful to have six people who call me their daughter.

Editors come in all shapes and sizes, and I'm grateful that mine—Sharon Pearson—knew all the right ways and places to press and prod so this work could take shape into something worth a reader's time, energy, and attention.

And last, but certainly not least, my husband Matt, whom I've only ever called Matty, so I do hope he recognizes himself in the pages that follow. This book—and this life—couldn't have happened without him. I'm grateful for his willingness to meet on the couch every night, the unofficial editing, an almost comical kind of optimism, and the kind of love and support that makes me think I can do impossible things.

To all of you with love and gratitude.

Colette Potts
First Sunday of Advent 2017

Preface

When the rector of the church I serve as theologian-in-residence first approached my wife about leading our Sunday school, Colette was a bit ambivalent. It was only a modest proposal for an interim position; our church school director had resigned after Easter and we needed just a bit of leadership to carry us through the remainder of the school year until summer and the search for a new staff member. Colette has been going to Episcopal churches since she was a child, so she was familiar with the Scripture and traditions of our denomination. But her profession is as a family therapist, not a children's minister. She was concerned because she hadn't had any training in scriptural interpretation, the history of the church, or the tenets of Christian doctrine. "I'll just try to teach one thing," she said to me. "Love."

I thought to myself, "There is no other commandment greater" (Mark 12:31). And I thought to myself, "Upon these two commandments hang all the law and the prophets" (Matthew 22:40). And so I said to her, "I think that's just what the church needs."

Colette had about three days to prepare for her first Sunday. Given the rush, she didn't have a lesson plan, specific Bible story selected, theological theme to convey, or even another volunteer to help. All she had was eight or nine skeptical children and forty-five minutes to fill while the grown-ups sat in church during the first half of the Sunday service. Intuitively, Colette began with the foundation of our faith and boiled it all down to Christ's greatest commandment. She gathered the few children together and she spoke about loving God and our neighbor, explaining that this was Jesus's teaching. She asked what love looked like and felt like to them, who they loved, and who loved them. She listened carefully to what they said and then asked who needed love and how they might share some love with those people. Lastly, she distributed colored paper, markers, paste, and scissors and helped the children make little love notes and greeting cards that read, "Somebody at St. Barnabas loves you." With these in hand, they wandered around the church parking lot leaving their love letters on the windshields of some randomly (and some not-so-randomly) selected cars. The children were delighted, thrilled at the anonymity, gratuity, and whimsy of their little gifts of love, amazed that they could so simply and truly follow Jesus. When they were done spreading their love, they entered the sanctuary together and joined us grown-ups for communion.

After church, back at our parsonage that abuts the church parking lot, Colette told me how wonderful the morning had been while I looked out our window as a few final congregants left coffee hour and returned to their cars. I remember seeing them smile, chuckle, or even wipe a tear from their eye as they read the notes. I remember watching them tuck the notes with tenderness and thanks into the pockets of their handbags or their suit coats. Colette's few weeks as our children's minister quickly turned into a few years, and during that time she developed the Love First program our church now uses, described in the book you now hold in your hands.

I teach theology and ministry at Harvard Divinity School and serve as a priest in the Episcopal Church. Since seminary I've been thinking seriously, practically, and theologically in settings both pastoral and academic, about the work of faith formation. Much of the best and most interesting thinking in this regard has focused on the latter term, on the idea of what formation is. But what Colette's program leads me to consider—as both a theologian and a pastor—is how we might rethink the former term also, and reimagine what faith is too.

We have faith, we assume, when we believe something to be true. When we say in our creeds "I believe in God," what we think we mean is, "I believe that God exists." This is fine, so far as it goes, but this notion of belief—of belief as the acceptance of a certain set of facts—is not only what faith can be. The Greek word *pistis*, usually translated as "faith" or "belief" in the English New Testament, means something more like trust than factual agreement. Former Archbishop of Canterbury Rowan Williams has even suggested privately replacing the words "I believe" in our creeds with "I trust" when we recite them. I wonder what the impact for our faith might be if, when we say, "I believe in God," what we mean is, "I trust God."

This is not just a rhetorical question. It cuts right to the core of what our creeds and covenants mean, I think. Trust is a behavior, and so it must bear out in the communities we build, the people we serve, and the manner by which we live our lives. This is why the Baptismal Covenant of the Episcopal Church marries our creedal statements of belief to corollary promises of love, support, community, reconciliation, and relationship. On the covenantal terms of our baptism, it's not enough just to agree to some facts. To trust in God is to live as a Christian, and the covenantal promises of our baptism, when taken together, affirm this. Building faith in Christ, building Christian community, and building God's just kingdom are all intimately and necessarily related.

This is what the Love First program has intuited since its first Sunday: that beginning with love is beginning in faith, that building faith in children means building trust in them too. It means trusting that their experiences of love are experiences of God, and then giving them language from our tradition with which to express those holy moments. It means trusting that their urge to serve is a work of the Spirit, and then giving them the opportunity to act and feel like the disciples they already are. It means trusting that their questions and confusions are signs of serious faith, and then inviting them to explore the complex stories and teachings they have inherited on their own terms. Though this program covers less of the Bible than some others might, I believe it is more— not less—biblically based. What it forms in children is a relationship of trust with Holy Scripture rather than a mere familiarity with Scripture's stories. This trust accommodates the questions and challenges children face, as they grow far better than any simple biblical literacy. Though the program uses a light doctrinal touch, I believe it is more—not less— firmly founded on Christian teaching. What it cultivates in children is a deep trust in God's love rather than rote dogmatism. This trust invites authentic, even courageous, theological reflection. Open and honest, it both welcomes and weathers the uncertainties of belief that all people encounter as they grow and change in faith.

The truth is, in only a few hours each month, we cannot teach a child all the answers she will need with respect to Christian doctrine, Scripture, worship, and ethics. The tradition is too complex, the demands of modern life too unpredictable. What we can do, however, is to show our children, in word and in deed, that our Christian teaching is a description of God's love; that our Christian Scripture is a testament of God's love; that our Christian worship is a celebration of God's love; that our Christian ethics is an application of God's love. We cannot give our children all the answers, but what we can give them is this trust in God's love. We can teach our children to trust God and themselves and one another. We can teach them to live their lives wholly in that trust. And then we can wait for the good faith we have fostered in them to lead them to the answers their lives and their loves will demand.

The Rev. Matthew Potts, PhD
Associate Professor of Religion and Literature and of Ministry
Studies, Faculty of Divinity, Harvard University
Theologian-in-Residence, St. Barnabas Memorial
Episcopal Church, Falmouth, Massachusetts

Introduction

Truth be told, when I was in my twenties, religion wasn't very appealing. I wasn't sure how my brand of church was any different from the others that seemed to have gone off the deep end. Organized religion—particularly Christianity—appeared to have morphed into something much different from what Jesus had envisioned. Church looked like it was about accumulating wealth, creating beautiful buildings, and excluding others—all things that Jesus openly condemned.

Even though—a couple decades later—it looks like some parts of Christianity are *still* a ways away from the core teachings of Jesus, I can say that after wading through some of the baggage the church brings, I've discovered some invaluable things that are almost impossible to find elsewhere. At its best, church is a unique setting that opens its doors to people of all ages, literally from birth to death. And it accepts these people in all forms, from the joyful to grieving, the lonely to the overwhelmed, the sick to well, the rich to poor, the entitled to the marginalized. You can be introverted or extroverted, hardworking or lazy, chatty or quiet. Any way you are or feel, church can be home to you.

Church became increasingly attractive after I had children. I worried a lot about how I was going to raise my children, what communities I wanted to surround us, and what my children would learn by the places we went, the things we did, and the people we called "friends." I spent many nights around the dinner table making a case to my children about why gratitude was important, only to realize that our conversations about gratitude really only happened in the first three minutes of dinner and almost always involved vegetables. I sensed this wasn't going well for us.

I had a hunch that if I didn't work hard to make our family's values clear, then I might be overrun by the things our culture values: competition, success, consumerism, and personal fulfillment. These are the values I feared would trickle into my children's hearts and brains, and weasel their way to the top of *their* list of priorities. If I wanted it any other way, it was becoming clear I'd have to work at it.

Before I became director of children's ministries at Saint Barnabas Memorial Church, I was a parent who spent Sunday mornings wondering what her children were doing in Sunday school and how it related to our everyday lives. The wife of a religion professor and one of the clerics at Saint Barnabas, I spent evenings asking clarifying and needling questions about the historical context of how we arrived at the religion and church that we see today. I asked Matt on a routine basis, "Is church *trying* to make religion irrelevant and confusing to children?"

All of these ponderings and conversations were aiming to uncover whether or not I could get what our family needed from church: something that increased the volume on love and kindness and drowned out the less desirable values of competition and consumerism that were seeping into our family's culture when I wasn't looking. The church should be the logical place for a family to find the support they need to raise caring, loving, and compassionate children. The church proclaims the teachings of a man who preached (a lot) about love and caring for the marginalized. If our family was coming to church on a routine basis and it was still unclear to my children what church was meant to be, then *our* church—at least—had some serious self-reflection to do.

The Self-Reflection

I'm a trained family therapist and was working as an in-home therapist when I decided to take the position at Saint Barnabas. I practiced several different models of family therapy, but my favorite was—and still is—the solution-focused model. It might sound redundant, since you'd assume all forms of therapy would be *focused* on a *solution*. But that's not necessarily the case. This one spends almost no time unearthing the root of the problem, and instead looks ahead toward solutions for arriving at a desired outcome. More importantly though, this model is built on the assumption that every person or family can generate solutions to their own problems; they might just need a little nudge.

That's how I've always felt about our church: *we have everything we need*. Too often churches are searching for the magic pill that's going to reinvigorate their children's program and bring back the families who've stopped coming. The remedy might be a curriculum, a climbing wall, or a bouncy house. If you buy it, they will come. Looking elsewhere for the quick fix can distract you from looking inward within your own congregation for your very own solutions to your very own problems, a solution that binds together the whole community.

Millie, my seven-year-old daughter, has a favorite, though clunky, saying that often rings in my ears, "Be yourself. Do not be your friend." It takes a few seconds to figure out what she means by this. "Be *yourself*. Do not be *your friend*." When Millie writes this on birthday cards, bookmarks, placemats, or the refrigerator, I'm not sure if she knows how desperately most of us need to be reminded of this. Millie's motto easily applies to all forms of envy, including the envy that some churches have for those congregations which appear to have it all. We're all guilty of peeking at what the neighbors have and feeling like we want that same thing, even if we never gave it much thought prior to fifteen seconds ago. Our church was guilty of that, and we briefly contemplated ill-fitting ideas, because duplicating someone else's program seemed a whole lot easier than the process of self-reflection and reinvention. We didn't want to hear that the best solution was not *their* solution, but *our* solution. That seemed like a lot of work and no one knew how to get there. To me, it felt like we didn't have much choice; enthusiasm for our children's ministry was quickly evaporating.

This is the story of our mid-size Episcopal church's struggle to reach today's young families. The process of self-reflection helped us locate the intersection of the needs of children, families, and the church. We took a risk to rethink (completely) how we teach children about God, religion, faith, and the church in a way that is meaningful to children, families, and our faith community today—and in the future. We erased our preconceived notions about what we thought we needed, we recy-cled the old curricula, emptied the rooms, and moved forward with one single commitment: make it all meaningful. What resulted was a program that the whole church was proud of, one that children and parents loved and teachers wanted to teach, and a new way of being that breathed life into our congregation. We finally had what we really needed. And we did it ourselves.

When word spread that our program was growing *and* that there was enthusiasm among children and parents—two highly coveted things in the world of children's ministry—other churches started inquiring. It looked to some like we were sitting on the golden ticket and everyone wanted a copy of it; whatever lesson plans or resources I could hand over would be greatly appreciated. In my first conversa-tion with Church Publishing, I told my (now) editor that I didn't have anything, really, to offer these other churches; this was not something to be circulated in an e-mail. This was, instead, a new model of chil-dren's ministry, one that would have to be nurtured and fostered by the whole church community. Churches would have to be *all in* if this were going to work.

This book is for churches who *want* to be all in because you know, too, that your congregation has the gifts it needs to reinvigorate the life of your children's ministry and the life of your church. Or, as they say in the field of family therapy: you believe that your church can gener-ate solutions to its own problems.

Our program assumes that children already experience holiness in their lives; likewise we assume the experience of God is authentic in our community and our families. God is already here. The love is already here. The solution to our problem is here, in our church and in our personal experiences, rather than in techniques that a prepack-aged curriculum might deliver.

That might be bad news for someone in search of a quick fix.

The good news, though, is that your community is full of golden tick-ets, too. Without having been to your church, I know it is rich with wis-dom and experience. It is full of people who don't have answers but want to search, who are willing to admit mistakes, who have suffered loss, who love and are loved, and who are prepared to participate in a chil-dren's program that promises to give back to the whole congregation.

Introduction

Our children's ministry is for the whole church, not only because the whole church benefits from a thriving children's program, but also because the whole church *is* the children's program. The people who will breathe life into your children's ministry are there, and perfectly situated to have a profound and positive impact on the children of your faith community. Whether unique or commonplace, the gifts of others can deepen relationships and connect the most unlikely people in the unlikeliest of ways; you need only nudge them into giving what they have to offer.

Your church is full of love waiting to be unearthed. Your job is to look for it in the unlikeliest of places, and give it a little nudge. Love first, and you'll find that others will too.

CHAPTER 1

• •

Our Challenges

Many churches today are facing unique challenges compared to their counterparts a generation or two ago. While some have managed to tap into the energy of children and families, others haven't moved far beyond a time when church was the only option for Sunday morning gatherings, still using the same model yet wondering where all the young families have gone. For previous generations, church didn't have to try so hard; families had more free time and there was more social pressure for families to attend church. That social pressure extended to volunteering, too, with fathers running committees and mothers teaching Sunday school. As we all know, for churches today that's no longer the case. Instead, families—barely recognizable to older generations—have changed, and churches have entered the competition for getting onto the calendars of young families—and not always making the cut.

If you've ever gone to any child-friendly event, you'll notice immediately that it is full of energy and excitement. From school concerts to soccer games to baby lap programs, children bring with them a kind of liveliness that is difficult to replicate. And when you don't have it, you tend to notice. And when you feel like it should be there but *isn't*, it can feel like emptiness or loss. Many at Saint Barnabas were feeling like we had lost something by not having more children in the church, and the only thing that would fill that void would be children themselves.

The joyful noise of children is great, of course, but everyone knows you can find that at the nearest playground or by a hosting a free kid-friendly event in one of your church spaces. I wanted that joyful noise to come from children who were connected to us in a meaningful way, those who felt at home in our church, and whose families felt supported by our community. I wanted to take that long view, the slow and steady approach to offering something that *really* resonates with children, their families, and our church.

I wasn't preoccupied with recruiting families or growing our program; that was never a primary goal of mine. Instead, I focused my efforts on integrating the children who were *already* part of the life of our congregation: those children I knew to be the kind, caring, and loving children that we wanted in our midst. If others were feeling like children were missing from our church, my first step would be to prove that the children we wanted were already here.

A New Brand of Busy

This is no easy task, even with the families already coming. Families are experiencing a new brand of busy that has profoundly changed the way they function and—for some— hugely impacts their relationship to the church. In addition, families are becoming increasingly complex configurations with single parents, blended families, and families being far-flung from extended relatives. Some churches are finding it impossible to answer the question they continue to ask themselves, "How do we reach young families?"

As a young—and busy—family ourselves (you know, the household with a four-week stack of unopened mail on the counter), I find it hard to believe the future of the church hinges on my ability to get dressed and to church on Sunday mornings. That's too much pressure, too much desperation, and evidence that the church doesn't get us. Instead, I want to focus on a solution. I want to talk more about what today's families need from the church, and how the church can start doing more of it.

Once upon a time, church was a lot of things to a family, a social hub being chief among them. Sunday school was a lively place for children to gather and parents weren't overly concerned with the content, just that their children were occupied while the adults attended church. Today, most families can fill their social calendar in many other ways, connecting through children's activities like hockey, Boy Scouts, or dance. They have located their own social center and often don't need a church to serve that purpose.

So what does or should church mean for these families?

If we think church is merely a social circle of sorts, then it might not be useful to most busy families today. If, however, we believe it offers much, much more—which I do—then it's not on such a perilous path as some think. Perhaps we just need to rethink what we do best, how it fits into today's busy world, and then do it really, really well.

Even with a steady decline in recent decades, some families are still here—week after week—expecting something from church. Several of our young families race down the hallway ten minutes *after* Sunday school starts, pulling on church clothes over running clothes, or brushing the dirt off their pants from an early-morning trip to the stables. Despite it (almost) always being easier to stay at home, on the bike path, or at the horse ranch, families still turn up.

Although the busyness of many families is mostly self-inflicted, it does serve a purpose that's not unrelated to the decline of church attendance. Families fill their days and weeks with things they need and want, things that give their children opportunities and experiences that shape them into the people we hope they'll become. For many, it can feel like a full-time job trying to develop children into well-rounded adults.

Weeks after I took this job, I decided to rethink children's ministry and what we were doing with children on Sunday mornings. Were we doing something that was worth a family's time and effort? Was the church offering its best self to children? I wasn't sure we were doing either of those things and feared we weren't even meeting the needs of the few families who kept coming, expecting something from us.

My first step was to challenge this notion that "The Busy Family" is the immovable object affecting the church. Perhaps churches no longer understand today's families. Or at least, maybe that has *something* to do with it. It got me thinking about the intersection of church and busy families and whether or not there *was* an intersection. I wondered if church had something more to offer these families on the go. Was there something here that needed tending by the church? I wondered if the church could offer something to families they *couldn't get* elsewhere, something they might consider adding to their hectic schedule, and maybe—I don't know—something they desperately *needed.*

What if families came to church and found that it actually made raising good, kind children just a little bit easier, and then raced to add it to their schedules like a coveted, hard-to-get-into summer camp? What if they found it absolutely necessary—a must have—for parenting in this jam-packed world? What we know about busy families is that they're busy because they turn up when it's something they *really* need or want. They're there. In fact, they're *everywhere*, which is why they're so darn busy. So maybe the problem isn't, after all, that families are just too busy for church.

Maybe the problem is that *church isn't offering what they need or want.*

Challenges for Families

I started asking parents about the challenges they're facing when it comes to raising children. Was there something families don't get from drum lessons, swimming, art class, lacrosse, dance, basketball, hockey, or ballet? Working as an in-home family therapist, I had become accustomed to this idea that every family had a struggle of some sort—some mild, some catastrophic. So it was altogether natural when I asked parents how things were going in their family in a real, I-mean-it sort of way. How were their children coping in school? How does their family spend quality time together? How does their busyness enrich *and* detract from family life? It surprised me that most of these conversations ended in the same place: families are busy, like *super* busy, and despite the long list of enriching activities, parents were left wondering if they were raising the caring and generous children they had hoped.

One mother quietly and dishearteningly whispered as our six-year-olds played together, "I'm afraid I'm raising a spoiled brat." A surprising number of parents asked with a look of hope in their eyes, "Can you find a soup kitchen where we can volunteer? I think that would be good for my family."

I understand these families' predicament. We had gotten into an unpleasant routine ourselves, using the first three minutes of dinner to deliver lectures on gratitude after fielding complaints about what was being served. These rants were award winning and often included stories of our own childhoods ("in my day . . ."), famine in South Sudan, the war in Syria, and children living in poverty down the street. Our children—in turn—had gotten into a routine of their own: glazed stare, exaggerated sigh, and an eye roll to await the passing of the evening harangue. This exchange wasn't what eventually bothered me, though; I'm perfectly happy giving talking points to my children about things of importance (isn't that called *parenting*?). What bothered me, in the end, was that these were the *only* conversations we were having about gratitude. And I wasn't certain that these moments were going to turn my children into the kind, generous people I was hoping. And I don't think an afternoon in a soup kitchen will fix it.

I asked families why that quintessential soup kitchen experience was important to them, and parents told me that they wanted ways for the whole family to do service for others in need, to make it a bigger part of their family life. One mother told me she was tired of merely dropping her children off at activities and wanted more opportunities to *share* experiences as a family. Another parent confessed that the suffering of others goes unnoticed by his children, and this bothered him—a lot. And most of all, parents told me that they were trying to raise children who were good kids, who cared about others, who were generous and grateful, and who were appreciative of the blessings in their lives. It just wasn't happening despite the best intentions. And they needed help.

As it turns out, these parents' instincts are right: they *do* need help. Between the time of these playground conversations and the writing of this book, I stumbled upon a collection of data that painted a grim picture of the children we think we're raising. Harvard's Making Caring Common Project published a report, "The Children We Mean to Raise," which exposes a trend toward children's prioritizing values of achievement and success over values of caring and kindness; high achievement is their priority, and more than 80 percent think it's ours too. In a survey of ten thousand students, three to one agreed that parents would be more proud if they got good grades than if they cared for people in the community. Children and youth are choosing their own achievement over caring for others, and they think that's what we want for them, too. Despite *almost all* parents intending to prioritize caring and kindness, this is what our children are hearing.[1]

---

1. "The Children We Mean to Raise," The Making Caring Common Project of Harvard Graduate School of Education, https://mcc.gse.harvard.edu/files/gse-mcc/files/mcc-research-report.pdf (accessed October 4, 2017).

This is a problem. Not only does it mean that most children are being raised to think that their personal fulfillment and achievement trumps caring for others, it means that we—as parents—are partly to blame for our children's missing the message that we *think* we're sending. This failure to communicate doesn't just mean we're not as effective as we think we are; it actually puts our children at risk for many forms of harmful behavior, including being cruel, disrespectful, and dishonest.

The best intentions don't always lead to the best outcome. As a family therapist, I find "communication problems" often top the list of concerns between parents and their children. Parents make assumptions that their intended messages are those that are delivered, unaware of the gross miscommunication that's happening, or how to rectify it.

This failure to communicate about values is bad news for everyone, the church included. Children are at increased risk, parents are missing the mark, the church's ability to offer moral development is seriously questionable, and our society at large is faced with children and youth who are not on track to becoming fair, just, and caring adults.

We shouldn't be surprised. If we fill our children's schedules with activities and classes aimed to make them happy and high achievers, then maybe they *are* actually getting the message we're sending. And maybe the problem is that our hopes are unrealistic that our children would put a high value on something we don't appear to value ourselves.

Challenges for Children's Ministry

Maybe as a holdover from times past, our children's program was still trying to *deliver* content to children. Our job was to keep children busy and entertained until they were old enough to go to church, or to stay home and watch themselves, and whatever curriculum we were using was not important or compelling to parents. The problem with this model is that we treat Sunday school like school, or merely a time for adults to teach children something they don't know. This model might work educationally speaking, but not pastorally. Assuming that children come to receive information misses an opportunity to minister to them in a real way, and neglects to help them be the ministers that they are, with a real capacity to relieve suffering. Sunday school should not be *just* about learning, but about being disciples of Christ, to love

6

and serve others. And we should empower and encourage children to do this work by first believing that they can.

Unfortunately, the challenges of creating a thriving children's ministry are multi-faceted. It's not simply a lack of enthusiasm and an absence of families. Even if the children are here, there are other obstacles to a successful children's ministry; finding volunteers can be a huge task. For some reason people *really* don't want to teach Sunday school. If coerced, some might help, but rarely does someone willingly and eagerly volunteer. Even our best teachers didn't answer the general call for volunteers—*they* had to be persuaded, too.

Based on conversations with current teachers and those who elected to participate in other ways, there were reasons why no one wanted to teach Sunday school. At Saint Barnabas, our schedule of Sunday morning services can be a drawback to finding committed teachers. We have an eight o'clock service with no music that mostly serves people without children; it's a more traditional service, and at Saint Barnabas this is more appealing to an older crowd. Our ten o'clock service with music tends to attract families. Children are dropped off by an adult at 9:45 (usually their parents, but grandparents are becoming increasingly influential in their grandchildren's faith formation) and remain in the classrooms for the first half of the worship service, joining the adults at the Peace and announcements around 10:45 when the whole congregation participates in the Eucharist. Asking a congregant to volunteer in the classrooms necessarily means you are asking them not to go to a portion of their regular church ritual. This schedule makes the calculus to volunteer much different from volunteering for other ministries.

This regular commitment aside, most people think a Sunday school teacher should be a highly qualified, skilled education specialist and a biblical scholar of sorts. In our church hardly anyone fits that description, which might explain the lack of interest; who would volunteer for something they felt grossly unqualified for? It was a problem if the loving, kind, and generous people of our congregation felt like they weren't qualified to be Sunday school teachers.

I was hoping to find a children's curriculum that even the unlikeliest people might love to teach: one that fit our budget, appealed to children, *and* made it easier for parents to add to their busy schedules. The curriculum I imagined would look to young adulthood, anticipating what lies ahead for children as they grow, and it would help develop a solid foundation for when their belief in God gets more confusing, complicated, and challenging. Anyone who has passed through adolescence knows it can be rough at times; the more positive supports, the better. This practice of anticipating needs of children and families is crucial and something the church should be in the habit of doing. The church needs children, but we need them as young adults, too, not only as a safeguard against the church's decline, but because church is something for a lifetime: from baptism to burial. If we ignore anything in between, we're likely missing something.

Saint Barnabas needed to learn how to be *more church*, figuring out how to tend to the in-between: children, their families, and the challenges they face today and in the future. Figuring this out is worth it, because children offer an energy and enthusiasm to church that cannot be found in any other age group. If you want what children can bring, you actually need children.

I searched high and low for the place where the needs and gifts of children, families, and the church intersected. It seemed logical to find that *exact* space where everyone complemented the other, and then build a program to tend to it. This was not to save the church, or even parents. It was because children need something from us: to belong and be included, to be accepted and be loved. What the church should be offering children is exactly that: a safe place where they are loved, even if they don't always feel lovable; where they feel included, even if they're not sure why; where they belong, no matter what; and where they are given purpose and where their presence matters, even at a young age. All of this is necessary in a community that not only includes but *celebrates* every generation and stage of life. School and home are not always the haven that children desperately need. Church can—and should—be that place by tending to their struggles as children in authentic and loving ways through a commitment to one another in our faith community, to God, and to the greater community.

CHAPTER 2

....

Our Leap

I took this job in the midst of a presidential campaign season that was historically toxic. Reading and watching the news left me feeling extremely disheartened about humanity as a whole, and I worried a lot about the world in which I was raising my children. News articles, advertisements, and social media were congested with hatred and a lack of compassion and empathy; the volume was loud.

I couldn't keep up with the barrage of depressing news stories, each story inviting me to contemplate a solution to the oppression and injustice swirling around me. Are we missing policies, laws, or practices? Do we need better education, affordable health care, or a higher minimum wage? What could get us back on track to *wanting* to take care of one another, to seeing others as we want to be seen? What the world was missing then seemed perfectly obvious. We needed more love. Plain and simple. Love for self. Love for others. Love for the earth. Love for those we know, love for those we don't know. Love for those we like, and even love for those we don't like.

And the church should be the place to find it.

This should sound familiar to us as Christians. The church is built around a man who preached—a lot—about love: loving God, loving ourselves, and loving our neighbors. He said to him, "You shall love the Lord your God with all your heart, and with all your soul, and with all your mind. This is the greatest and first commandment. And a second is like it: You shall love your neighbor as yourself" (Matthew 22:37–38). Jesus likely said this over and over because we *needed* him to say it over and over. And though some things have changed in the last two thousand years, it seems there's still a need to preach about love, over and over. It seems to me that if you are seeking a place where you feel loved, it should be overwhelmingly clear to children (and adults) that the church is where you can find it.

But I fear it's not.

Somewhere along the way we've started complicating the message, letting children go to Sunday school for years without a full understanding that being part of a faith community is about loving and caring for others. Instead, children walk away thinking that church and religion are about complex, sometimes unrelated Bible stories, donuts, or doodling on the welcome cards.

Imagine Something New

My husband, Matt, and I spend a great deal of time talking about church, children, and church *and* children. Even before I took this job, we fantasized about how we wanted our children to spend Sunday mornings, which often included ways for our children to apply faith and God in meaningful ways to their everyday lives. When the opportunity arose to try something new, we combined my background in curriculum design and family therapy with his expertise in religion and the church, plus his love for understanding complex theology and my love for a more simplified one. I didn't want to get distracted by so many other things that can detract from a children's religious program and—quite frankly—an entire church community. I imagined something new, something we hadn't seen before. And something we all needed *and* wanted. If we learned anything from Harvard's Making Caring Common Project, it's that our children need us to be *direct*: no beating around the bush, no overcomplicating the message, just keep it simple. As Christians we are supposed to be about caring for all God's creatures great and small. How could we do more of that in our faith community?

At best, children are in our Sunday school classrooms for one hour a week. According to the Pew Research Center study that surveyed families about their participation in religious organizations, children are in church for an average of only one to two hours a month, which means only a handful are with us each week.[1] Imagine how many hours a month children spend watching television, playing video games, or even sitting on a bus to and from school. Are one to two hours a month—or one hour a week for the superstar attendees—too much for talking about loving one another?

Of course not.

Whether children are new, irregular, or regular attendees, it's crucial that the message be crystal clear. At the end of each hour, children should know that coming to church is about gathering to love and to think more deeply about how we show love, why we exhibit love, and to whom we share love. *This* is not complicated, so let's keep it that way.

Through the lens of love, we wanted to address the challenges families face to raise loving and caring children, help them recognize the importance of cultivating a culture of empathy and compassion in their family, and prove to them that our Christian community could be an integral part of that process. We wanted families' conversations about church to be grounded in a shared commitment to serving others in need, and that a drive to help others would be an integral part of their family's church experience.

Research is telling us that developing empathy doesn't happen on its own; parents' behavior places a value—whether high or low—on how empathic children turn out to be, and a community who commits to caring for others can have a lot to do with it. Our churches should be providing this caring community for children and families, not only because it serves our need and desire to grow, but also because this is what it's meant to do, and it's more urgent than ever.

• •

No matter where your church is, how long it has been there, or what the size, I know one thing it wants more of: children. Longtime church members will love telling you of the glory days when their services

---

1. "Religious Landscape Study," Pew Research Center, Washington, DC (2014), http://www.pewforum.org/religious-landscape-study/attendance-at-religious-services (accessed October 4, 2017).

had lots of young people and teens and families interested in all things related to getting a Christian education. In my last call at Saint Barnabas, children were mentioned as important to the life of the parish, but two things frightened me: there was no money set aside to hire a quality director, and the family service met in a different place, away from everyone else in church!

When we decided to hire from within our parish, it was easier to take risks. Colette said she would direct the children's program, but only if it could be different than it's always been. I knew we had to do something radical, so I agreed wholeheartedly.

The first thing we did was get rid of the old curriculum and find out what parents really wanted. Their answers led to "Love First," a program based solely and entirely on love.

It sounds so simple, but if you're reading this book and see what happened, you will realize it was profound. For me, as the rector, what we saw happen at our parish was an answer to our prayer. Children—and their parents—started coming to church and their friends followed. People wanted to teach, and our coffee hour grew to a light lunch so families did not have to rush out. And everyone of different ages got to know each other—to love each other.

And isn't that what Jesus wanted? To love each other and to find God through that love. —The Reverend Patti B., former rector

• •

What we imagined for children was that our church would feel like home, that when they enter the church or the classrooms they would notice familiar faces and feel connected to others and to the place, and know—for certain—that their presence mattered. We wanted this for everyone—not only children and families—and we intuitively knew that the way that could happen was to find ways to connect children to other adults in the church in ways that really mattered.

It's tempting to peer over the shoulders of other churches, looking for the secret to attracting families and keeping them interested. For many it's an urge toward making church fun, a quick fix.

That disinterests me profoundly; I'm not motivated to make church fun in order to attract attention. Church is where we bury our loved ones, mourn their absence, and long to be with them again. Church is where we find ways to address the profound suffering of others, including deeply troubling issues like war, poverty, addiction, and prejudice. It's where we come to grieve a loss so profound it feels like it might swallow us whole, to talk about it in hopes that it doesn't, and to find people who can provide us the support to bear it. There is nothing fun about any of that, and we should not pretend that it is, or that it ever will be.

It's also the place where we celebrate the most cherished moments in our lives: births, marriages, deepening our relationships with others. It's where we can express joy and gratitude for the many gifts we've been given. It's where we can be ourselves, in all our vulnerability as human beings. It's a place that's meant to help us be our best selves. I wouldn't necessarily call that fun either—I'd call that important. And a faith community—the Church at its best—does that really, really well.

We didn't imagine creating a program and a place where children always felt happy; we imagined creating a place where they felt alive. This place should not be *a* place, but *the* place where we let children bear all that life is throwing their way, and make it clear that we are the place where it fits just right and that we are prepared to help them through it.

The church often excels at gathering people together and socially connecting them by virtue of regular gatherings and shared experiences. Children are no exception, and eventually find themselves connected to other children they see on a regular basis, doing projects and crafts together that form bonds of friendship. And at our best, we offer children something that interests them, keeps them engaged, and makes it easier for parents to get them there on a Sunday morning.

• •

There are many striking elements about the Saint Barnabas children's ministry program. This is not a curriculum that Sunday school teachers teach to children; it's more like an approach to living in community. The program has clearly worked as a way of welcoming people into a faith community who hadn't necessarily been in one before.

This approach is not an intellectual exploration of faith. It gets down deep into what children are drawn to, how they thrive, and how families

thrive. This children's ministry is about love. The Saint Barnabas children's program has had a ripple effect in the parish and has brought a
deep-seated sense of hope to the parish. —The Reverend Louise F.,
Interim Priest

• •

The church hasn't always been great about offering content that's
directly relevant to children's lives today, that enriches the rest of their
week, and positively impacts their relationships in other contexts. The
church seems to miss the boat on invigorating the complex lives of
today's children in a meaningful way.

When rethinking our children's program, we imagined a program
that could address all the anxieties and stresses of children today, the
problems I'm called to help families address as a family therapist. We
imagined a program that would give children tools to apply their religion and their relationship with God to overcome these challenges by
having honest conversations about bullying, divorce, death, peer pressure, insecurities, and worries. We imagined children learning that
church would be an appropriate place to voice these concerns, and
that they could learn ways to cope with these stresses, formed by the
best of what Christianity has to offer.

We imagined a program that acknowledged the gap in moral development that parents suspect and research confirms. Despite feeling
like church is not relevant to their lives, there is a place that it can
and should be relevant to families, to tend to that space that is being
filled by the louder voice of consumerism, achievement, and personal
gain. Not tending to children's moral development is having a negative impact on children and our society as a whole, paving the way for
greed, cruelty, and injustice. Church, it seems, is more relevant than
ever to young families, if only we could figure out how to do it in a way
that *works* for today's families.

Is there a way to address our challenges, generate our own solutions, and dig deep into our own Christian tradition to do it? Could
we simultaneously tend to the needs of children, families, and our
churches in a simple and meaningful way? Could we do this by offering
what the world desperately needs right now?

In the pages that follow is our church's leap to rethink how we could tend to the needs of children and their families, and how other churches could better serve families in meaningful ways. We set out to think more deeply and exclusively about love: following Jesus's commandment to love our God, our neighbors, and ourselves. We wanted to do this in a way that considered how children are loved in our space and how our spaces love us back; how our community can spread love in large and small ways, but always in authentic and honest ways; how a love for one another encourages the entire community to share their love in new ways; how the love of our community extends outward to those who need our love and our help more than ever. This is all that Jesus asked us to do. This whole place, this whole community should be all about love. So let's put love *first*.

And the rest can come later.

CHAPTER 3

. . . .

Our Sacred Spaces

Before we had children, Matt would often take me on tours of churches whenever we found ourselves in a new town or city. The inside of these churches never surprised me and always left me feeling a little bored and impatient. Even so, I would kindly wait until he was done doing whatever he had to do while I looked forward to stopping for coffee on the way home. I never understood why Matt wanted to visit church after church knowing he would find *exactly* what he'd been expecting, and only a slight variation from what he'd seen in every other church. It was only—years later—after I *stopped* expecting something different that I found comfort in finding things nearly the same in each and every place. Now when I walk into any church anywhere in the world, I look for the familiar things, the things that tell me *this is church*, a sacred place that someone put a lot of love into.

Churches are good about this and know how to do it instinctively and intuitively; Sunday morning worship wouldn't happen without knowing how to care for a sacred space. Our altar guild spends countless hours each church season readying the altar, polishing the silver, cleaning the linens. Our ushers methodically straighten the books and pick up whatever's been left behind in the pews. Dropped crumbs from altar bread are carefully picked up by hand and disposed of in a special way, along with any leftover wine. Clergy, acolytes, and choir members are dressed in special attire before they approach the altar. Candles are lit and snuffed with steady hands and special tools.

In sacred spaces there's rarely excess or extra of anything; we have only what we *need* in that space, and everything there serves an important purpose. You won't find a half-dozen crucifixes leaning next to the altar, or a pile of broken candles in the front pew. The seasonal dressings for the altar are not piled in a corner, but tucked away neatly, ready for the next season. Everything is neat, tidy, and put in its place, ready to welcome us upon our arrival.

The Church Welcomes You

The Episcopal Church has an easily recognizable sign that almost always includes something like "All Are Welcome" or "The Episcopal Church Welcomes You." On many of these signs, those are the only two pieces of information on the sign, which means welcoming is important to our church. Welcoming, though, does not simply mean that you're *allowed* in this space, or that you won't be turned away. It means: this place is meant for you, and we are eager and ready to receive you.

If you have small children, upon entering a church you recognize immediately if the space has been prepared for them. Until recently, our church space at Saint Barnabas gave the impression that it was designed for adults; children were tolerated in the sanctuary but belonged in the Sunday school rooms. Churches should pay attention to how they welcome children, finding ways to go beyond *allowing* or *accepting* children, and moving toward a readiness *to receive* children.

Our church sanctuary is essentially one large room with very little space to hide if you need to get away. Side aisles don't exist for an easy exit, which is a potential challenge—or nightmare—for anyone with small children. There is only one hiding spot in the church, which is an alcove at the entrance to the church where the ushers stand to hand out bulletins or the choir congregates before processing. There is a rocking chair that has lived in that cramped space as long as I've been here, representing a genuine attempt to be child-friendly. I've been offered this rocking chair on many, many occasions over the course of several years and have found it useful only once or twice; either my children were inconsolably wailing (and the rocking chair was still too close to the church sanctuary), or the winter temperature made the unheated rocking chair space mighty uncomfortable. Although this chair is *always* offered with the best of intentions by some of the most loving adults in our congregation, it simply doesn't meet a family's needs and doesn't acknowledge that we know what those needs are.

Our church has limitations that present challenges to welcoming young families and small children. This is the reality for many churches, but it doesn't make it impossible to rejuvenate lifeless spaces or make little tweaks that make a huge difference. To address some of these pressing needs, a self-appointed committee of concerned and committed mothers (new and old) was formed to assess our church campus spaces and whether these spaces were welcoming to children.

• •

Pure joy is what I see on the faces of our congregation just before the Peace when the children enter the sanctuary in search of their parents. They sprint into the Holy Space knowing they belong and—gleefully or with great seriousness—search the pews. As senior warden I often catch the eyes of our older members who are smiling and nodding, appearing to be genuinely proud and happy. They, like me, are probably remembering many years ago when churches reverberated with loud and boisterous children and then gradually became silent.

This welcoming and joy didn't happen by accident. It was carefully grown and nurtured. We stopped talking about all the reasons why no children came to church (competition from sports schedules, parental exhaustion on weekends, parental disinterest in formal religion) and instead focused on the invitation. We built a playground, rehabilitated the Sunday school spaces, and refurbished bathrooms. We added baby-changing tables to the men's bathroom, too.

And most importantly we hired a director of children's ministries. Sunday school is a ministry of love and acceptance, of learning and sharing, all of which must be in the DNA of the individuals involved. So it has been at Saint Barnabas.

Many of our elders have been invited to share their gifts and memories with the children and loved doing so. Parishioners are proud to see the quadrupling of church school membership. Children run around the parish hall visiting new friends, both old and young. Attendance at the quarterly children's services did not shrink but grew!

Saint Barnabas is a church in transition. Soon we will be calling a new rector. Normally transition can be fraught with splintering, factions, and grumbling. I credit our children's program for helping us avoid these pitfalls. A willingness to change by absorbing and welcoming new families seems to be the prevailing emotion. —Sue D., Senior Warden

● ●

The Bathroom

Children (and their parents) have specific needs and these often relate to the bathroom. If you have a child in diapers or who is midway through potty-training, you know that mornings can be organized around bathroom breaks; easy access to the appropriate facility can make or break your experience. You also know that having a place to lay down your baby and wash your hands is crucial. These things are obvious when you're the one who needs them, and almost invisible to those who don't. This is an ongoing challenge for places like churches that try to welcome people of all ages and stages of life. One of the first steps to making Saint Barnabas more family-friendly was to toss our old, wobbly changing table with a stained fabric cover and replace it with a wall-mounted changing table in the women's—and men's—restrooms. These little changes are easy, fast, and relatively inexpensive but speak volumes about a church's commitment to caring for the needs of the youngest parishioners.

When Sam, our second child, was baptized at six months old, Millie was two years old and in the middle of potty training. I remember this being incredibly stressful for all of us because we wanted his baptism—and the potty training—to go well. All precautions were taken, and fingers were crossed that Millie would get through the ninety-minute service without needing to use the potty. When she announced she had to pee (of course this was going to happen), I knew we couldn't dress ourselves for the wintery day, walk to the nearest bathroom in the neighboring building and back to the sanctuary in under fifteen minutes; if I took Millie to the bathroom we'd miss the baptism. With a lot of reluctance, I ignored her request and hoped for the best. She whimpered a little and then—surprise, surprise—peed all over me, and the two of us celebrated Sam's baptism soaked and wet.

While the property committee and vestry deliberate and debate about the cost of tinkering with a historical building in a historic district, we have to do what we can to make nature's call a little less inconvenient for those who are with us today. That meant cleaning up the old bathroom in the basement of the sanctuary (the one no one told us about), and making it a usable space for children. Because of its location, there had been a general consensus to forget it even existed: "Let's pretend it's not there, and direct people fifty yards across the parking lot to the updated bathrooms." Imagine that's your only option, and *then* imagine the knee-jerk reaction to your four-year-old announcing he has to go to the bathroom in the middle of winter, midway through the service. For me, this was almost too much to handle, and if I were required to dress my three small children and leave the building, it meant the morning was over for us.

This logistical hurdle meant accepting the extra noise and movement from our children in the sanctuary if we wanted them present. For us, this was key. We simply don't have the kind of space that allows for easy exits and minimal disruption, and every parent of a young child has noticed—and stressed over it. Instead, we have to welcome the noise that comes along with wiggly children and parents who can't easily slink into the background. If we don't, young families will not feel welcome in our midst, and we've been unwelcoming to people we really *want* in our community.

Worship

The biggest and most immovable obstacle at our church, I think, to welcoming families with young children is the distance from our church sanctuary to our classrooms, fifty yards away in a separate building (with the updated bathrooms). Understandably, this can make new parents uneasy about leaving their child, or nervous children uneasy about leaving their parents. For the foreseeable future, though, this is an obstacle that can't be remedied, so in our congregation, at least, we need to be flexible and take extra care to make families comfortable in our space. As I mentioned, for Saint Barnabas, that has meant letting young families with antsy children linger a little longer in the sanctuary when their instincts are telling them to cut and run.

Years ago when Millie and Sam were both under three, I found myself in one of the back rows of the church, basically wrestling them away from the incredibly fragile books arranged exactly at their eye level. Week after week, I'd see other parents across the aisle wrestling their own children away from these books, perhaps bribing them—as I was—with sweet treats after the service in exchange for mediocre behavior. I'm certain my children ate 90 percent of their lifetime desserts in the hour that followed the worship service, all negotiated in the pews with stern whispers. Without getting to know each other beyond the back row, we parents developed solidarity and camaraderie that ranged from sympathetic glances across the aisle to silent, exaggerated gestures of, "I'll stay here and watch the rest of your kids while you take that one to the bathroom." Without knowing it, this Back Row Gang (as we affectionately called ourselves) gave each other permission to stay in the pews when things got hairy, or to run—and often trip—directly in front of the pulpit (our only exit to the basement bathroom) with a child, shout-whispering, "Mommy, I have to pee!" As you can imagine, this is embarrassing and something you desperately hope to avoid, but is not always possible when you have children.

This also meant that—like it or not—we became a part of the church experience for everyone else in the church. The other adults who sat near the back rows grew to love our children and reassured us that our children's squawks and giggles brought them joy. This encouraged and empowered us to stay despite our inner voices telling us to make a run for it. We didn't feel like the church space was ready or prepared for us, but everyone within arm's reach offered a kind of solidarity that was comforting and supportive enough to keep us in the pews.

Learning Spaces

Churches are good at protecting their sanctuary and preserving its holiness. It's intuitive for most of us, even if we're not experts in church design or liturgy; we can easily detect when something is out of place or doesn't belong. If there were clutter or disarray, you would immediately sense that something was amiss. This is in stark contrast to other spaces in the church. If you've ever opened a church closet or cupboard, you know what I'm talking about.

It's not a mystery why this happens to shared space. These areas are both lacking ownership *and* owned by the masses. Throwing things away doesn't feel like anyone's responsibility, nor does it feel within anyone's purview. For our classrooms, that meant an accumulation of a lot of things that may or may not have been useful—perhaps ever— and were never purged because either no one wanted to do it, or no one felt like they were allowed to.

If learning spaces were treated as the sacred spaces they are, they too would remain clean, tidy, intentional, and inviting—just as the church is—or should be. Unfortunately, our classroom spaces left something to be desired. They had become repositories for all things related to children or religion. Broken toys littered the nursery and religious books with inappropriate messages crowded our bookshelves. These items had accumulated from the good intentions of members who wanted to give our children and teachers more resources and materials. But these items were a real chore to purge. Much of this stuff was shoved into closets and onto shelves, piled into cabinets and corners, leaving our classrooms looking more like a crowded thrift shop than spaces for learning. Not only did this make it impossible to do the work that's meant to be done in those spaces, it sent the message that those spaces were not sacred and not being cared for in a real way.

An important part of children's ministry is tending to these spaces, ensuring they're sacred, and encouraging children—and everyone else—to treat them with the same reverence as the sanctuary. These spaces should always be purposeful, intentional and welcoming to all. We want it to be obvious that these spaces are loved, and that the people in these spaces love one another.

Let's commit to readying our spaces for the people we hope to welcome, giving our time, attention, and love to the spaces in which we gather. Welcoming doesn't happen simply because we want it to; it happens when we are deliberate, intentional, and do what it takes to make it happen.

De-clutter

Oddly enough, the first step to rethinking our children's program was to clean out all the classrooms. Despite the state of our house for the eight years since we've become parents, I don't like clutter. I can't even think straight in a disorderly space, and while I might be at one end of the spectrum on this, I know that an untidy space is directly related to how well I'm able to work. As our classrooms had become dumping grounds for donated supplies of any kind, things would mysteriously appear when no one was looking. This resulted in disorganized, chaotic spaces that lacked clear intention and purpose, not to mention it was impossible to know what we had and where to find it.

My first few months in this position, I spent a great deal of time working on the classrooms, as a crucial step to answering the questions: Who are we? What will happen in these classrooms? What will the children learn?

In the end, I emptied every single classroom, put the contents in the hallways, recycled a half-ton of useless paper materials, and requested that all the old furniture be unscrewed from the walls—even the shelves couldn't hold normal-sized books. When it came time to return the useful materials into the classrooms, there was no clutter at all. In fact, there was hardly *anything* at all.

Clutter is distracting and cumbersome, and can quickly detract from—instead of enhance—a space. It's difficult to keep it clean and organized, so it often ends up dirty and disorganized, both of which are unacceptable in a sacred space. Beth Teitell from the *Boston Globe* published an article, "Today's Families are Prisoners of Their Own Clutter," about the stress that clutter is causing families, and how the abundance of possessions is actually decreasing the quality of time spent in our spaces.[1] It turns out disorder is not only physically distracting, but emotionally and psychologically too. This is true at home,

---

1. Beth Teitell, "Today's Families are Prisoners of Their Own Clutter," *Boston Globe*, July 10, 2012, https://www.bostonglobe.com/lifestyle/2012/07/09/new-study-says-american-families-are-overwhelmed-clutter-rarely-eat-together-and-are-generally-stressed-out-about-all/G4VdOwzXNinxkMhKA1YtyO/story.html (accessed January 22, 2018).

at work, and even at church. This should come as no surprise, given that Marie Kondo's *The Life-Changing Magic of Tidying Up* is a *New York Times* best seller and a part of everyday conversation. Many people will tell you their take away from this book is to touch every object and only keep what brings you joy.[2] While a good approach for your own personal space, it gets slightly more complicated when dealing with a space designed to accommodate a group of people. Teenage Mutant Ninja Turtles bring me no joy, but for some reason they make Danny, our three-year-old, really happy. So they get to stay.

It takes time to weed through spaces to make them entirely welcoming, but it is important to *find the time*. Make sure everything visible is relevant because it sends a strong signal about what takes place in that space. When it came to our classrooms, it was an easier task to allow back into the rooms only what was useful to the children and teachers for their time together. As it turns out, we didn't need much. Humans make snap judgments about how they feel in a space within a few seconds, and parents bringing their children to a church classroom are no different. It will be difficult to convince a family of your winning curriculum if the spaces don't reflect a sense of respect and love and that a great deal of care has been put into welcoming the children who will be learning and loving in that space. We were quickly able to pare down what was in our spaces, and—little by little—they became increasingly sacred spaces by sheer virtue of the care and deliberation that was being put into them.

Safety

Beyond the church's safety requirement and guidelines that include having multiple adults present with children and having windows in doors, it's important for churches to continually think about how to make a space safe for children. Church is where sensitive topics are likely to arise, more so than in other contexts. We are the place where death and suffering are part of our community and we routinely tend to both. Children should feel that anytime they gather in a learning

---

2. Marie Kondo, *The Life-Changing Magic of Tidying Up: The Japanese Art of Decluttering and Organizing* (Emoryville, CA: Ten Speed Press, 2014).

space at church, there is an implicit safety that allows for discussion of whatever might not come easily to most children, or might not be appropriate in other places.

One of our teachers, Jackie, has high enrollment in her class and so has two rooms available to her: one with tables and chairs, and another with a very large carpet. Upon this carpet with children, she says a prayer, reads a story, and allows for (sometimes extended) discussion about the topic of the day. It's not uncommon for Jackie's class to spend twenty to thirty minutes talking about socially isolated children, bullying, peer pressure, a loved one who has died, or confusion about gender norms. You can hear a pin drop during these discussions; these children understand that this is a space for sharing and for comforting, and they feel compelled to do both.

I joined Jackie's class for a Magic Carpet session—as she now refers to it in our discussions—and listened intently as an eight-year-old boy shared with twelve of his church friends that he was being teased in school for "liking things that girls like." He shared with the group that his feelings had been hurt, and that this had been really upsetting to him. A seven-year-old friend, not usually known for his softer side, turned to him, patted him on the back, and said, "You know, I would never do that to you." And the eight-year-old responded quietly, "I know you wouldn't, I know you wouldn't."

I don't think I'm overstating the importance of a place like this for children, for a place to share these difficult things, and also a place to have your softer side shine. Children are routinely sharing with Jackie about the difficulties they experience in school, and this is the safe place where they feel supported, encouraged, and empowered. Jackie actively fosters a sense of safety by talking explicitly about the importance of loving others, modeling loving interactions, and taking notice of micro insults and teasing that—if left alone—leave children thinking that this is acceptable in our spaces, and can result in making our sacred spaces less safe.

The physical space, too, is a key component to what Jackie is able to do. These conversations don't happen in the hallways or on the playground or at coffee hour; they happen on the Magic Carpet, the de-cluttered room with one large carpet signaling that this is a space for sharing and listening. Jackie will tell you that something special happens when they walk into that room, close the doors, ring the bell, and say a prayer. The children are different, the conversations are different, and the sanctity of the space has so much to do with it.

Visible Cues

When you enter a church, you can often tell what season it is by the color of the altar hangings, or the variety of flowers around the church. In our church, potted lilies signal Easter, purple cloths signal Lent, red cloths for Pentecost. These cues are important to the church sanctuary, and I believe they're equally important to our learning spaces.

This is also true for what projects children take home. We don't always feel compelled to send children home with something they've produced on Sunday morning. Sometimes, children do carry home the products of their morning, but we don't choose activities based on what children will show their parents. The work that children are doing is sometimes best used to present to others in our congregation or to be left on display in the classroom. We underestimate the importance of these cues to giving parents—and other adults—a fuller sense of what is happening in our classrooms. Every opportunity to share what children are doing with the rest of the congregation should be taken.

We also think deeply about what visual cues we give children who enter and stay in our learning spaces. Only a select handful of posters or paintings are on the walls of our classrooms, intentional cues to the kind of space we are creating and what can be expected to occur in this space. Paintings with "God is Love" and the Golden Rule are largely displayed in every classroom because these are important components to each and every gathering, sometimes used by teachers and children as a gentle reminder for empathy and compassion, even with each other. We also display a poster that reads "Be Brave, Choose Love" because choosing love sometimes takes courage. We want children to know—right off the bat—that we know it can sometimes be challenging.

You'll also find on our walls: "Where is God in this?" and "How is this inspired by Jesus?" For us, the prominence of these messages is crucial to making connections between what we are doing in these spaces and why it is important to our Christian community. The repetition of these questions (and frankly, the repetition of the response) gives children confidence to talk about God and Jesus in ways that are relevant to our morning activities and in ways that make sense to them.

Every classroom purposely has the same signs, posters, and banners on the walls. These are not questions, words, or phrases that children grow in and out of. We start these messages with our youngest class and continue through our oldest class, even hoping they'll seep into the grown-ups who share our spaces every once in a while. Our program tries to anticipate a time when young adults don't find religion relevant, important, or meaningful in their lives. Sending these consistent and timeless messages is important for children today, and for the young adults they are soon to become.

Shared Space

It's a luxury to have dedicated classroom space, and not all churches are so fortunate. If your space is shared, that doesn't mean that it can't serve everyone's use in a deliberate way. And if you have dedicated space, that doesn't mean that you shouldn't share it with others. Children's artwork and projects nicely displayed in a library or meeting room add to the holiness of any space, and other church committees or outside groups can learn a lot about what the children are doing by sitting in their space for their monthly meeting. We try to leave the rooms ready for others to gather throughout the week, and I regularly encourage groups to consider our space when looking for meeting locations. I want everyone to feel welcome in our rooms and find that they are inspiring and pleasant. This must mean that they're always ready, as any sacred space usually is.

Quality versus Quantity

You'd be hard-pressed to find a stack of processional crosses anywhere in the church. Instead, you might find one or two of high quality that are given a place of prominence and used on a regular basis. There simply isn't a need for more than that, and more would only get in the way.

While cleaning out the classrooms, I sorted through more than a thousand crayons, most of which were broken. It seemed like a no-brainer to purge any coloring utensils that stifled inspiration to make beautiful art. I kept a huge bin of all the intact crayons of highest quality (those freebies from the Italian restaurant had to go), but noticed that—for some reason—children still didn't like using them. Maybe there's something about the bin of hundreds of crayons—even if unbroken—that feels a bit like a pile of dirty laundry; the more, the messier, and the less inspiring it will be.

If you're on a tight budget, this is not necessarily bad news for you. If you opt for low-quality crayons, for example, children don't feel inspired to color. And in some cases, they simply won't. Millie begged me to buy high-quality gel pens for her Sunday school classroom, and I did so after patiently waiting for them to go on sale. Children have *loved* these writing utensils and care for them in markedly different ways than the crayons and half-dried-out markers. These pens immediately took the place of every other writing instrument on our shelves, and—in the end—we spent the same amount on supplies for the year.

When thoughtfully whittled down, most of the materials for any class can fit into a closed cabinet and bookshelf. That should be the goal of any learning space despite your situation. This is great news for churches that share space, because it means other dedicated space can be used for learning spaces, with those spaces having the capacity to accommodate more children on Sunday morning because there are fewer materials taking up valuable space.

To maintain the quality of our materials and to avoid being overwhelmed by the quantity, we've enlisted the children's help in weeding out any materials that are broken, damaged, or not working; for some reason, they love this. They enthusiastically and diligently throw away dried-out markers, set aside books with ripped pages, and ask for tape to rehang artwork that has fallen down. They have been empowered to care for their materials and be part of maintaining quality over quantity, and they take this responsibility seriously. And seriously, it's pretty neat to watch.

It Takes a Village

Our church literally has teams of people who care for it. The altar guild, the sextons, and the property committee comprise a multitude of people who tend to our buildings, grounds, and the details of readying the church for services. This is not a job for a handful of people—it takes a village. The children who use them, not simply the teachers or me, should also tend to our classrooms.

Matt's mother and my grandmother are of Japanese descent. We're both smitten with Japanese culture and—although not perfect—we find some parts of Japanese society and culture profoundly superior. In Japanese schools, classrooms belong to children, not necessarily to the adults, and children are expected to care for their spaces in ways typically reserved for cleaning staff in American schools. Japanese children wash floors, move tables, empty the garbage, and take out recycling; they work as an industrious team to clean up whatever just happened in that space and prepare it for what's happening next. This is their space, and they know it. Japanese classrooms are a microcosm of Japanese society at large, everyone feeling like they're an important part of caring for common spaces. Matt's brother lives in Tokyo with his family, and his sister-in-law Kiwa casually remarked—as she was doing laundry—that she empties her seven- and twelve-year-olds' pockets before sorting laundry because they're often filled with garbage picked up from the commute home. Compare that to our American children, who proudly take a service field trip to pick up trash from the beach, even if their school playground is littered with trash.

Japan, as a whole, fosters this responsibility in children, making it clear—at a young age—that everyone contributes to keeping things running smoothly. Something is lost when we tend to sacred spaces in secret without involving children in the process, or by letting them think—or assume—that it's an undesirable job meant for other people. Children's participation is not *only* useful (usually), but it's crucial to giving them ownership of the space, making it clear that they are part of making it—and keeping it—sacred for themselves and for others.

Much like for our classrooms, I wanted our family's sacred space to stay neat and tidy, but there didn't seem to be enough time in our day. At every turn, I'd use that time for something else: a more expansive project, a longer book. Picking up Sam's Legos one evening at home, obsessively sorting them by color, it occurred to me that my children love their toys and that picking things up didn't have to be the dreaded chore that I'd thought. We tend to our house and its contents because we love it and want to care for it; this is an important part of being grateful and being good stewards of our space. It feels less like a chore and more like a privilege when we think of it like that. One evening I was cleaning the kitchen while Matt was in charge of getting the kids to clean up the living room, and I overheard Sam saying, "I didn't make that mess, why do I have to clean it up?" (Not an uncommon utterance.) Like a well-trained deputy, Matt responded, "I didn't ask you to clean it up because you made the mess, I asked you to clean it up because we love our house and want to take care of it."

This works. Not only for our children, but also for us. This was not only the summer that I made the kids clean the house every evening, it's also the summer I cleaned out the junk drawers.

How Sacred Spaces Treat Us

There's no doubt that we treat our sacred spaces as if they're, well, sacred. Their holiness demands from us respect, care, and love. In turn, these sacred spaces give us something back: a space where we are welcomed, where we feel at home, where we feel loved. In family therapy, we use the term *circular causality* to describe the dynamic of two emotions or behaviors that seem to be both the cause and the effect of the other. Sacred spaces are part of a similar feedback loop: the more you treat it with love, the more love you will feel in that space and the more you will love it. Which started first or which followed second is not really relevant or important anymore. What's important is that it's happening, that there is a whole lot of love there.

I am constantly walking the halls of our church buildings and around the church campus, asking myself: do children feel loved in this place? The answer, of course, must *always* be yes, because feeling loved is part of feeling welcome. But perhaps the more important reason they should feel loved in this space is because it's essential to encouraging them *to love* in this space; feeling loved makes it easier *to* love.

CHAPTER 4

• •

Our Precious Hour

Once word spread about the success of our children's program, I spent more and more time meeting with people from other churches, helping them find ways to revitalize *their* programs. Some were interested in the concept and how we came up with it, others quickly jotted down notes about the projects and activities we'd done. As one meeting ended—and it was clear this woman was leaving with a bulleted list of project ideas—I told her apologetically, "If it looks like this is all about the activities, then I've not done a good job of explaining what we're doing."

A successful activity doesn't make a successful program. It's *more* than that. It's about critical self-reflection and looking more deeply into what your church has to offer. Are there opportunities to foster empathy and compassion through unlikely relationships? Is there a belief that your church is full of all the gifts it needs?

Our first year was guided largely by my gut, tempered by a whole lot of counsel from Matt, and informed by my experiences as a mother, educator, and family therapist. We did a lot of flying by the seat of our pants, making adjustments to add or drop things as we went along. These conversations with other interested congregations helped me revisit the process by which we designed our program and the rationale behind every move we made, making it easier to explain and easier to share.

The overall principles of our children's program are clear and easily found on our website and any piece of advertising material; no one was requesting to meet because they were uncertain about the program's values. What people *really* wanted to know was, "What does that *look* like?" Despite my lengthy descriptions of how our classrooms are run, a handful of people from nearby churches still wanted to *see* what was happening in the classrooms during our precious hour with children on Sunday mornings.

If you were to join us, here's what you might notice:

Every class has a rhythm that is followed almost every Sunday morning of the school year. This is crucial for creating a safe space for children of every age. We protect this rhythm like it's the base recipe for your favorite muffins: a small amount of tinkering is fine, but stick to the basic recipe or you don't get muffins.

There is a tendency to skip over some of the seemingly less important steps in our Sunday morning, but I would strongly urge you not to; they're all essential. The rhythm of our classrooms is our ritual for gathering, the prayers are our liturgy, and we keep to it like a worship service: it's the same every week, except for special occasions. It might surprise you to hear that the only component that can be omitted on the fly is the activity or project. On some of our best days, classes will spend their precious hour praying, sharing, and listening. We should always be in the habit of protecting what is sacred about our precious hour, and it's not necessarily the craft project.

This routine is crucial to cultivating the kind of environment that children need from us. So much so that we have it displayed on the wall of every classroom and most look like this:

Welcome and Arrival

Circle Time: Mindfulness Bell, Prayer, Check-In, Lesson,
    and Discussion

Project or Activity

Sacred Space TLC

This is not just for teachers, but for children and parents. We hope it sends the message that these are the components we believe to be invaluable in creating a space that is loved and one that encourages children to love.

Preparation

Prior to children's arrival, teachers take fifteen to thirty minutes to prepare the space, lay out project supplies and books, and write verbal cues on the white board. Children know to look for these clues when they arrive, indicators of what they'll be doing that morning. When children arrive, teachers should be *waiting* for them, not making last-minute preparations. This is important not only for children, but for parents who are saying goodbye at the door. They, too, should have an idea about what will be happening during that hour and feel that their children are ready to be received.

Welcome and Arrival

Children are dropped off in classrooms at 9:45, and parents walk to the sanctuary (in another building about fifty yards away) for the 10:00 worship service, while children spend approximately one hour with their classes. When children arrive at the door their teacher greets them. An intentional greeting is a teacher's first interaction with a child in that precious hour, and it serves to let them know, "I'm grateful you are here."

As children arrive it's helpful to have them start on an activity or quietly work on something while the teacher greets other children as they come in. Some of my favorite moments with children have been sitting around the table immersed in undirected conversation waiting for others to arrive. This is time for connecting with children and helping them connect to one another. An anxious child (or parent) will notice if a teacher is prepared to pay attention to children. For younger classes, and depending on class size, this might mean having the second adult in charge of getting children started and settled while the lead teacher welcomes the newly arrived. Whatever creative solution works for your church and your classrooms is perfectly fine, just so long as this moment is protected and preserved.

Depending on the age group, the opening activity can be a variety of things but should always be something that makes for easy transition. If it's a project that children feel compelled to complete, children arriving late will have difficulty moving on. Our younger class will often play with puzzles, play dough, or animal or people figurines on the rug, which is an easy way for new children to get acquainted with others. For many of our classes, we use "Praying in Color" sheets, which are essentially "adult" style coloring sheets designed for children.[1] The purpose of these activities is to have something for children to focus on when they arrive. Like sitting in a quiet church or listening to the music before the service begins, they help everyone prepare for what's to come.

Circle Time

Gathering

After about fifteen minutes of arrivals, teachers transition their classes to the lesson and discussion portion of the class. The younger classes do this on a separate rug, signaling that their attention is turning toward one another and to the teacher. The older classes don't have a separate rug, but their room is constructed in a way that is always readied for discussion with low coffee tables and floor cushions. This time always contains the following things: a moment of silence and mindfulness, a prayer, check-in, story or lesson, and discussion.

The Mindfulness Bell

At the beginning of each year, children learn how to love and care for their bodies by learning how to rest, using different forms of mindfulness to calm ourselves when needed. Many of our children learn about mindfulness in school and are familiar with different ways to do it. I like that we're able to connect what they learn in other contexts to what they learn at church, making our Sunday mornings further relevant to their everyday lives and vice versa. Each gathering begins with the ringing of a Tibetan singing bowl, and the children know to be silent and still while they wait for the ringing to stop completely. We never intended to do this every week of the year. It was something we started in September and was so well received and anticipated by the children that we never stopped. For some, it seems to be the highlight of our time together.

---

1. Sybil MacBeth, *Praying in Color: Drawing a New Path to God* (Brewster, MA: Paraclete Press, 2007). MacBeth's website also offers downloadable coloring pages and templates: https://prayingincolor.com.

Prayer

Years ago, when I first started teaching Sunday school, my predecessor, Dorothy, told me that she always started with a prayer on the rug. I shadowed Dorothy for a couple weeks before taking her place and I was truly impressed with her spontaneous prayers that were so eloquent and so natural. I had no such talent for that, and it quickly became a massive source of stress on those mornings. Prayers can be heartfelt, beautiful, and touchingly personal; I wanted to offer such prayers but was certain I couldn't. I'm not a flowery writer, and I'm not a flowery pray-er either. I like outlines, even for prayers, and worried that mine would be too practical and methodical, and that the children wouldn't respond well to them.

On that first day, I meant to have a children's prayer book with me. It was by the front door and left behind as I was wrangling our one-, three-, and five-year-olds. Sitting in front of the children on the rug, I lamented the hours I'd spent finding the perfect prayer in that perfect book, and so just opened my mouth and let something fall out.

I have only one prayer up my sleeve and its lack of creativity turns me red with embarrassment. Even so, it always goes something like this, "Dear God, thank you for bringing me here today to spend the morning in this place with these children. I'm grateful that all of us are healthy enough to be here, especially Lauren, Sam, Nora, Bella, Gavin, Ciara, Grace, Collin. . . Please keep us healthy and safe this week so we can gather again next Sunday, and so we can do the important work of loving and caring for those who need us most. Amen."

This is not publishable prose, I know. It's the same every week, except for the names of the children, and it doesn't change—because I don't have any other ideas. The first time I mentioned the children's names, I was looking for filler, something to make my prayer longer. I was surprised to see the children straighten their bodies, some looking down at their hands, others staring me straight in the eye, but all clearly waiting for me to call them by name. By the third child, I could tell that the sixth couldn't wait to be named aloud.

Years later, I haven't changed my prayer one single bit. Every morning of every gathering I say the names of the children in a prayer, announcing to God that I'm grateful that they're here because *I am grateful that they're here*. Maybe it's true that I haven't changed it because I still don't have any other ideas. More likely, though, I keep doing it because the children understand it and love it, which still makes it the perfect prayer for us.

I tell teachers that they can say whatever clunky prayer they want, that it can be from a book or extemporaneous, but that it *must be done*. And what's most important—and not to be missed—is mentioning each child by name, taking the time to look them in the eye, and thanking God that they are in our presence.

In spite of my awkward prayer, I think there's an unintended benefit for children and teachers. Somehow and somewhere I got the impression that a prayer had to be perfectly long and eloquent to really count, and I brought this baggage to my classroom. Part of what we are doing in these moments is teaching children how to pray. Despite whatever combination of words come out, however short, long, or prepared it is, what's most important is that it's honest and authentic, shows care and love for others, and comes from the heart.

Check-In

For years we've said prayers before dinner in our home. This is not always a smooth operation, and we've gone through periods of resistance from whoever happens to be three years old, tired, or cranky. When Matt and I were deliberating over whose family prayer to use, I had only one condition, that whichever one we chose (we chose his), we must say it slowly enough to feel meaningful. I'm a stickler for this, and will make us stop and start over if I think it sounded rushed. No one at the table—except me—has ever appreciated this redo.

We've added something to our family prayers in recent years, each of us sharing something we're grateful for and something that's worrying us. We did this to make our prayers feel more relevant and meaningful, always working against the tendency of our prayers to become perfunctory. Since then, we've found ourselves praying for each other, our friends, family, and neighbors in need, and strangers affected by the most recent tragedy or natural disaster, using this as a way to check in about what's bothering us or lifting us up. When it became clear that Danny, our three-year-old, was going to pray for Syria each and *every* evening, I resisted the urge for a redo. The repetitiveness of his prayers is not a sign of complacency, as it turns out, but a desperate need to keep praying for what he cares deeply about.

• •

Most children go to church because of their parents. For us it is the other way around. We came to Saint Barnabas by way of our seven-year-old daughter, Madeline, less than a year ago. One day she asked us if we could take her to church and Sunday school (most likely because she heard the words from one of her peers), and we decided to indulge her curiosity. There was something about that first Sunday school class that resonated deeply within her and has kept her, including our family, going back every week. Perhaps that is a testament to the wonder of the children's program. We hear her tell us with delight what she learned when our family is reunited for communion but we also see for ourselves the group's engagement and work they do for the community during the children's services at Saint Barnabas. Not a week goes by without the gentle reminder of our Sunday morning ritual from our daughter but it neither feels like an obligation or a burden. It makes us whole and allows us to be together. To belong to a church that values inclusion in every way is truly amazing. —Sung Bin P.

• •

This opportunity to contribute something or voice a concern is important for our family dinners, and important for our Sunday school classes. Following our prayer, teachers leave space for children to check in, or share what is on their mind. No one is obligated to participate, but they *must* know that a space in our morning is dedicated to hearing what they have to say and that they can decide what to do with that moment. There's no end to how you can use this time, using a technique like our family's or something more open-ended. One of our teachers, Heather, has a ritual of going around the dinner table with her family, offering "one up, one down" to share one great thing that happened that day, and one not-so-great. What matters here is that there is time and space made to share and that children understand that their presence and participation matters to those gathered.

Lesson and Discussion

It doesn't matter how you present the theme of the day. Whether a great book, an appropriate Bible story, a skit, or puppet show, this is when you would do it. We have a running list of books that touch on themes like empathy, prayer, self-esteem, God, and courage, among others, and this list—and the books—are handy for teachers to use throughout the year. We also have a carefully selected list of age-appropriate Bible stories that guide our themes throughout the year, and as a program, we select one parable per unit and spend time learning about who was telling it, what each character represents, the historical context, and how this story is applied to our lives today.

There is no perfect way to deliver a story or lesson, but it must be age appropriate. All of our selected Bible stories take age and development into consideration, so children are being presented something they can reasonably comprehend. This is true for our book selections too; books meant for older children can frighten younger children, and longer books don't work for short attention spans. Read through whatever you're doing ahead of time, and skip pages that aren't appropriate or don't add to the conversation. It's not uncommon for teachers to have pages paper clipped together to make a book more suitable for the group. If a long book can be shortened to better fit your crowd or to make for more discussion time, then by all means go for it.

My children love to chat during a book. They have questions along the way and love to interrupt for clarification. Danny practically makes a game out of it, stopping midway through every sentence to talk about whatever catches his eye in the illustration, like the shape of the clouds or the color of a button on a little girl's overalls. If you welcome the interruptions, then pay no attention to what I'm about to write. If you're like me, and find the interruptions disruptive to your train of thought, then plan to read the book twice: once to get through it, and once to pause for discussion; just let the children know it'll be happening.

Our discussions are a hugely important component of our program. Whatever your style, pick a plan and then *plan to stick with it*; children will adjust to your routine and benefit from the predictability of it. Some teachers prefer to have their discussion while reading the book or story, seamlessly weaving the two together in response to the children's questions. This discussion serves two purposes: to talk more in depth about the content of the story and to pay attention to the language children are using. Teachers listen for the way children talk about themselves and how they talk about others. Thoughtfully and lovingly, teachers model the kind of language we promote at our church: a language of love and acceptance. Children are given the time and the prompts to imagine what it would be like to be different characters in each story, how they might have reacted similarly or differently, and how this story might remind them of something happening in their own lives. Children are invited to connect these stories to their faith by asking, "Where is God in this?" while the class looks for loving moments or interactions in each story.

One of our favorite books is *The Invisible Boy* by Trudy Ludwig. This story starts with a socially invisible boy drawn in black and white amidst a colorful page of other children.[2] The reader quickly notices that the invisible boy, Brian, goes unnoticed by the rest of the children. Ludwig skillfully spends a few pages showing this boy invisible throughout his school day. Only when a new classmate notices him does he begin to show signs of color; as he gains a full-fledged friend, he gains full color too. This is an exceptional conversation piece for our classes, for those who feel invisible, and for those who know of the invisible children in their school. We foster honest conversations about what we do sometimes that inadvertently hurts others, what a loving response would look like, how we can work to be more loving in our interactions with others, and where God is at work in all of these moments.

Teachers look for ways to praise loving gestures from the children, reliably encouraging them to be loving and caring in every interaction. We assume children seek praise and subconsciously calculate how to get it during this time and in this space. When we continually praise acts of kindness and love, they notice, and they do more of it.

Project or Activity

The project or activity is always something that reinforces the lesson of the day. Not every week can or will be the perfect activity because Sunday school class sizes fluctuate from week to week, and teachers don't

2. Trudy Ludwig, *The Invisible Boy*, illustrated by Patrice Barton (New York: Knopf, 2013).

know how many children—or which children—will be attending until the moment they walk in the room. Additionally, it's not uncommon for us to have sibling pairs that prefer to stay together, widening our developmental gap in some cases. Even so, we do our best to choose activities that children feel good about doing and are worthy of our precious time.

At certain times of the year, we do service projects that extend over a few weeks so that everyone gets a chance to participate; otherwise all of our activities can be completed within the hour. When choosing activities or projects we try to use high quality materials or something parents might want to keep; we try to avoid activities that are immediately thrown away. We often do projects that stay in the room to decorate walls or let people know what classes are working on. When children are especially industrious and make more than one craft, we encourage them to share it with someone sitting in a neighboring pew. Many of the children's projects have been given away as special gifts to other parishioners, connecting children to other adults and connecting adults to the content of our children's program.

Sacred Space TLC

As a teacher, I was guilty of prioritizing a fun project over time for cleanup, just like at home. I'd often leave the classroom in shambles, and make a point to come back later to clean up the mess. This wasn't ideal, but seemed reasonable to me given the time constraints of a Sunday morning. Following our first year and as a result of the conversations with other congregations about what we were doing at Saint Barnabas, I was better able to zoom out and get a bird's eye perspective of our program. And the messy rooms at the end of the morning were a red flag.

We'd spent a year prioritizing many other things, not taking into consideration the state of the rooms when we all headed into the church. I was left wondering what this said about how we loved these spaces and was afraid we were sending the message that we didn't really love them at all. We resolved to make cleaning up the final portion of our routine and as essential as the other components. One of our teachers, Katie, started calling it "Sacred Space TLC" (and now we all do) because this is exactly what we're trying to do: tend to our sacred space with loving care. Each Sunday morning, the final portion of our precious hour is tending to our space, loving it back, and preparing it for the following week.

Breaking Bread

Snack had always been a part of Saint Barnabas Sunday school, so much that it never occurred to me to do away with it in our first year. Some children were so attached to snack that I didn't want to take away their favorite part of Sunday school. Although, as Matt likes to point out, if snack is the highlight of your children's program, you've got some work to do. Instead of prepackaged junk food, I opted for a healthy snack: loaves of fresh-baked whole-grain bread, smeared with real butter and artisan jam. No processed food, no high-fructose corn syrup, and coincidentally no money left in my budget after three months.

I agonized over whether or not to keep the snack. Ever since Millie was a toddler, she wouldn't exchange a single word with visitors until we broke bread together. Like clockwork, after nibbling on anything with caloric content, Millie would hop down from the table a changed person; she was now ready to share toys and stories. I believed that there was something about sharing food together that was deeply spiritual, that altered the relationship in a real way. I thought this type of connection was invaluable to our children's program and desperately clung to it.

Our program had swelled so much in September that snack time no longer resembled the spiritually nourishing breaking of bread that I had hoped for. It looked more like a soup kitchen assembly line with children trudging through the line making demands, offering up complaints about what was being served, and comparing notes on who got how much of what. Meanwhile, we were diligently avoiding allergies, intolerances, and aversions, all in hopes of pleasing the children in front of us. It seemed the only thing about this experience that was worth preserving was my hope that it would someday be something different.

If your program overlaps with a time when adults are also eating, then you might want to consider having a snack. Or, if your program is small enough and you can ensure that it's done in a way that a prayer of gratitude, sharing, and cleaning up is all part of the experience, then I would consider preserving this ritual. But generally speaking, I don't think Sunday school programs need to feel compelled to use precious time with children to snack. Children *love* snacking, and will clamor for it if given the choice. But if it can't be done in a way that is meaningful, eliminate it. We discontinued it after Christmas break and no one even noticed. Except parents, most of whom applauded the change.

Every Moment Matters

Many of the children in our classrooms talk about the stress of being at school, particularly the social aspect of peer pressure, bullying, and other disruptive behavior in and around the school. It's difficult to talk about bullying without each child chiming in with his or her own experiences. Conversations with parents, too, are filled with their child's experiences and how bullying is affecting their learning, sleeping, or overall behavior. It's clear that despite our schools' best efforts to reduce this troublesome behavior, it continues to happen.

My children are not impervious to this either. With only a couple of school years under her belt, Millie has already had difficulty with peer relationships, and her stories—at least through the lens of a seven-year-old—have sounded a lot like bullying to us. This mostly happens on the playground, out of eyesight and earshot of adults, which seems to be a common scenario when parents gather to compare notes.

The bullying that's troubling so many children these days is the subtle behaviors that accumulate over time and leave children feeling unsafe, isolated, and powerless. Children can detect the spaces where cruel or unkind behavior goes unmonitored, leaving children feeling safe in some areas and profoundly unsafe in others.

We aim to cultivate a culture of love and kindness among our children at Saint Barnabas—and, in truth, among the adults too. That means we commit to paying attention to the smallest slights or put-downs that can accumulate over time. We want to avoid sending the message that we're only concerned about the *really* unkind stuff, not the *sort of* unkind stuff. Children will hear similar language from every teacher that includes noticing the behavior, offering reminders that certain behaviors aren't tolerated here, and why this is so. For example, if someone was teasing someone else, they might hear, "Those words are hurtful. We can't treat each other like that here. We want everyone to feel loved and safe in this place, and that can only be done when everyone does their best to act with love and kindness."

Reinforcing community standards to any child, when done correctly, benefits the whole group. Often children teasing are the ones being teased, or hoping to *avoid* being teased. Holding everyone to this standard contributes to everyone feeling safe, including—and especially—the child doing the teasing. We address this behavior because it's the loving thing to do, letting *every* child know that during our time and in our space, you are safe from this behavior. This matters, and children notice; either is reason enough to do it.

From time to time, behavioral problems arise. As much as possible, we avoid addressing these concerns in the way that children are accustomed to seeing. Punitive disciplinary actions are inconsistent with our theme of love. Instead, we reach out to parents, we lead with love, and we work together to find ways for children to participate in a way that doesn't compromise the safety and sanctity of the space for other children. When this happens, there are often underlying issues that expose a family's need for our help and result in a much-needed pastoral conversation. In other words, love first.

Identifying and addressing behavior in this way also lets children know that it's okay—even for adults—to have negative emotions of anger or disappointment without it changing how we feel about one another. Children can disappoint us without it ruining—or even changing—our relationship, rather it sets boundaries and expectations so we can feel safe enough to share, support, and love one another.

CHAPTER 5

∙∙

Our Curriculum

A children's ministry should do more than offer programming on Sunday mornings. It should offer children and families something meaningful, something that enriches their life, and something that deepens their relationship with God as well as their church community. If you're pondering the content of your children's program (and you should *always* be pondering this), it's helpful to take a holistic approach to examining what you offer and how it resonates with children, parents, and teachers and how it fits into the big picture—both in and out of church.

Reflecting back on my own experience as a Sunday school goer, I don't think it's an exaggeration to say I learned almost nothing in my entire experience with Sunday school or youth group. It pains me to say that, now that I know the difficulty of finding the volunteers to do it. The highlight was—hands down—the chocolate glazed donuts at coffee hour.

Looking back, it seems like the church I attended missed a golden opportunity to lay the foundation for what the church means, where it gets complicated, and how I could use God to get through the tough times that were on their way. When those tough times came, it *never* occurred to me to use my faith or the Christian community to wade through the muck. For me, it was quite the opposite. Those murky times coincided with a deep resistance to the baggage that religion carries, including the Bible. By then that sacred text had proven itself to contain words that were used to condemn some of the people I loved most, and so I discounted it altogether as something that was just a bunch of rubbish. And it took years to undo the damage.

I often joke about not being thrilled when asked to be a Sunday school teacher. Dorothy, the teacher in the preschool classroom knocked at the door of our house to see if I "had any ideas" about who could take over in her classroom. She and I pored through the church directory for more than half an hour before I told her, "I'll be in touch if I have any ideas." I didn't even realize she was asking me to fill her spot. Out of love for Dorothy, I became the new preschool teacher.

Improper as it might be to confess that I had deep reservations about taking the plunge, I do think it's relevant. I'm an educator and a family therapist who thrives on the possibility of helping families become stronger and healthier. My reluctance to teach Sunday school is worth pondering because it seems like I would be *exactly* the kind of person who would delight in a task like that.

The reason I wasn't interested is rather simple, though difficult to admit: I care a lot about helping families, but I wasn't convinced that the curriculum I was asked to teach *actually* translated to helping families. I didn't want to miss an opportunity with the children and families at Saint Barnabas. The risks are too high to deprive a powerful community that is founded on God's love for humanity and Jesus Christ's teachings to care for one another, especially those who are the most vulnerable. I couldn't settle for giving families what they expected; I wanted to give them something that they needed, but didn't know existed.

Every gathering your church has should be an opportunity to share or reinforce something important that relates to the overarching goal of your program. Each time children are in your midst they should better understand what it means to be a Christian, and what we are being called to do. Let's not ignore that families come to church because they hope to receive something important and meaningful for their family. We should make sure we give them just that.

Your curriculum and the resources you use should aim to relate to religion and faith as children grow. One of the oversights of many church curricula is that they don't plan for the future. Children will grow into young adults who eventually become the adults that may or may not remain in our pews. If we don't offer something more valuable to children and something that is relevant today *and* in the future, then we shouldn't be surprised when children stop coming once they're old enough to stay home alone on Sunday mornings.

Our Christian Tradition

Christianity was founded on Jesus's insistence that we are all loved by God and that we are all called to love and care for one another, *especially* the least among us. This is what children and families need—and maybe always have—and exactly what the church has to offer. Our tradition values community, individuals who are committed to supporting each other through celebration and grief. We acknowledge that to be human is to make mistakes, and we build in ways to forgive and make amends. We pray for each other, in hope that there is more to celebrate and less to grieve, and we sing together and share meals. Much of what we offer is rich with history, tradition, and ritual—all based on God's love for us.

We, too, have a comprehensive and complicated text, relied upon for generations of people to find inspiration, solace, and direction, to remind us of how Jesus's words and behavior shape us into the people we are today. The Bible is a holy text, guiding our Christian tradition for generations, in every part of the world. At best, the Bible is recognized as a valuable tool in understanding the relationship God has with God's creation and how we as the people of God live out our beliefs to make the world a better place for all. The Bible can be used well or used poorly. At worst, its complexity is ignored, opting instead for a simplistic interpretation of complicated events that really need informed contextualization for us to understand today.

By the looks of my recycle pile, our previous curricula were exclusively biblically based, relying on new and interesting ways to retell standard Bible stories. Many relied heavily on ease of use, opting for downloadable handouts for quick planning. On the other end of the spectrum were those that asked for investment in high-quality materials and training, not selling simplicity and ease for teachers, but children's love for things that are special and cared for.

When Millie had been going to Sunday school for about a year and a half, I asked her what she thought was happening in the classroom.

She said, "We sit on the rug, listen to a story, and then we drink juice." From a five-year-old, I expected a slightly more sophisticated interpretation of what was happening in Sunday school. I knew she had talked about Sarah and Abraham that day, so I made a point to ask, "What was today's story about?" She responded, "Something about old people having babies, walking somewhere. Actually, I have no idea."

I remember being confused—a lot—about Bible stories in Sunday school. Even as a child I found them complicated, unpredictable, and frighteningly violent: brothers killing each other, and God wiping out all the people on earth with a flood. This confusing and developmentally inappropriate delivery seemed like unnecessary clutter to me. That's not to say the Bible isn't important, but we've gotten in the habit of letting biblical literacy be the driver of children's faith formation. In other words, forming children to be familiar with Bible stories in lieu of forming children into disciples of Christ who love and serve others became the overriding principle.

Much like our classroom spaces, we wanted to de-clutter our spiritual and religious message to children, making it age appropriate and incredibly direct. Instead of the roundabout way we had been approaching Christianity with children, we wanted to respond to the pressing nature of our world stage. If our message is to love and care for others, the world needs that now. Right now. Our oppressed and marginalized neighbors need our children to be empathetic and compassionate today, and we should do our best to send them out into the world to do this important work. Now. Not whenever they get around to figuring out the complicated message we often give them.

Living with a religious scholar means several things: there are no simple answers to *anything* that relates to religion or theology; Karl Barth and Dietrich Bonhoeffer are household names; and a conversation about *really* complicated theology is perfect right before you want to fall asleep. Luckily, before I fell asleep one night, something sunk in.

It turns out there is someone of great importance and influence who believes that every single passage of the Bible should be interpreted as a message of love. Whether to take the Bible passages literally or figuratively, Augustine of Hippo said that God is love and so every Bible passage is one of love. If the literal meaning is *not* one of love, he says

47

we should keep looking until we find that message.[1] Augustine was a fourth-century Christian bishop and—as it happens—probably the most important theologian of Western Christianity. That's the Bible I want to teach: Augustine's Bible; the one that has us pressing through the typical messages that we deliver to children, and searching until we find the message of love. *That* is a sacred text.

The Bible can speak to our lives in a meaningful way, and all our churches—in worship and programming—should do that for children and for adults. Much of the Bible is complicated, and a difficult collection of texts requires spiritual maturity and critical wisdom to read well. Noah's Ark, for example, is important to our tradition and often used in children's programming. One of our teachers recalls lying awake at night as a child, wondering if God was going to come again to kill all living things with a flood. It's an important story, but not one that builds children's trust in God's love, and so might not be the best story to focus on with a group that still believes in Santa Claus. Better to build a foundation of trust in Scripture in these early years so later, when our children encounter these more difficult stories, they can do so on mature and sure footing.

Instead of focusing on the more traditional stories, this might mean building upon stories about justice and love that are often overlooked, such as Zacchaeus, the walk to Emmaus, or Bartimaeus (see Appendix B). It means rethinking the narrative of our "must-have" stories like Noah or David and Goliath. Our churches should not create obstacles to understanding our complicated text by trying to simplify popular stories that are considered mandatory in a children's curriculum.

• •

Like many other parents, I want to raise my children to be helpers and to learn the value of giving back to their community. When I heard about the curriculum for the Saint Barnabas children's program, I knew we had landed in the right place. As a family, we were less focused on our

---

1. Augustine's categories are literal, allegorical, analogical, and anagogical, but those distinctions are not pertinent to my larger point.

children learning biblical history; we needed another avenue for teaching them how to be kind and caring toward others.

With a focus of loving themselves, their neighbors, and God, I have seen my children blossom in Sunday school. They look forward to going each Sunday and were upset when it ended for the year. I never imagined that they would love going so much that they would miss it when it was over!

One of my favorite aspects of the church school program has been witnessing the intergenerational relationships between the children and our older parishioners. I love that the children often write to parishioners who may be homebound, ill, or in need of a pick-me-up. They craft cards and write hopeful messages and even get mail back! They have also created handmade gifts to share. Seeing an elderly parishioner's face light up when presented with these special tokens further strengthens my belief that we have found our forever church. I look forward to the boys growing with the loving support of their church family. —Jessica M.

• •

The parents in our program were not clamoring for biblical literacy for their children. They were asking for the biblically rooted *values* of Christianity to be instilled in their children—and in their family. They wanted their children to know the importance of caring for others in need, and that it was something they did as a family because it was important. The best way we teach the children in our program is by doing and sharing, with a careful selection of biblical stories to reinforce the message of love.

Moving away from a lectionary-based curriculum was not an easy decision. It meant bucking a long-standing practice in our children's formation, a trend that was in place for reasons I couldn't pinpoint. But when we looked more closely at the other parts of our tradition that are easy to overlook in a children's program, like ritual, prayer, and the practice of approaching the suffering of others, paired with what parents needed for their children and their families, the decision to make a radical change was rather easy. In fact, it felt like I no longer had a choice. We had to try it. Our Christian tradition has so much to offer that is directly relevant to children's lives today and to parents' desires to raise compassionate children; we just wanted to make it crystal clear.

Love First: Our Curriculum

Looking back, our program and its accompanying curriculum began to take shape while I was cleaning out the rooms, looking at all the materials and asking, "What message does this send to the children about the Christian tradition? Is this relevant to the lives of the children sitting in this room?" I found binders and handouts from a half-dozen curricula that had been used in some way, shape, or form over the past decade or so. The cabinets and bookshelves were jam-packed with posters and books focused on religious themes. Certainly, some of this unearthed treasure could be useful to us, right?

I did find a ton of materials, all that seemed sort of relevant to church and children, and sometimes only to church *or* children, but not much was relevant to *this* church and *these* children. Not all religious materials are created equal, and it can take some work to weed out the materials that send a message that doesn't resonate with your church, or conflict with the tone of your church's mission statement and vision.

The piles of old curricula materials were evidence that we had tried many things over the years, exploring curriculum after curriculum, hoping that one might stick. It made me wonder about the decision that lay ahead of me and how I would decide: which curriculum will be the best fit for the people in this place? I had deep reservations about having taken this job when my "to be recycled" pile had 100 percent of the old curriculum materials. Not a single thing seemed relevant, inspiring, special, or something that I could eagerly use with young families. The downloadable coloring pages of Bible characters, word searches using Scripture references, cut-and-paste Bible characters, all were designed to be easy for teachers but left *me* wildly underwhelmed. I wasn't looking for something I could sell to teachers as easy; I was looking for something that I could honestly describe to parents as important.

I reflected back on the conversations with parents—churched and non-church-going—about the challenges they were facing when it comes to raising children, and doing my own work to locate the space where church could better serve families. If parents need something a church can offer, we hadn't figured out what that was, or how best to do it. I also reflected on the pervasive reluctance to teach Sunday school and what that hesitance says about what we are asking people to do. I reflected back further to conversations with aging parishioners about their strong desire to have more children in the church or to feel more connected to the children who were already here.

What's particularly relevant to the church community is the Making Caring Common Project's findings that parents are quick to blame *other parents* for not prioritizing caring, thus making it difficult for *their* children to keep priorities straight. As it turns out, *most* of us want our children to be kind and caring community members more than we want them to be accomplished, high achievers; we just think we're alone. Gathering in a community formed around love and service to others makes it easier for parents to feel like they're *not* alone, that their children will be surrounded by other children who are getting the same message and by other adults who make caring for others a big part of *their* life, too.

One Precious Hour

Matt and I spent countless hours talking about the curriculum we were going to design. These conversations occupied the bulk of our time together for nearly a year because we knew our big ideas had to be whittled down into one single hour a week. One precious hour a week is all we have with children, and that's only for our superstar attendees. As I've noted, most children attend once or twice a month, with others attending even less than that. We thought it prudent for planning purposes to be realistic about that fact, and design a curriculum that made it clear—even in one class—what we were trying to do in this place. I became obsessed with these sixty minutes, de-cluttering that hour with the same intensity as I did the classrooms.

In that hour, we wanted to use a curriculum that was simplified and worthy of a teacher's time and energy. We wanted parents to feel like their children were getting something important out of the hour they spent with us, and it was worth the rigmarole of getting the family ready on a Sunday morning. We wanted children to spend that hour feeling like they mattered, that their *presence* mattered to the whole of us, and that the work they were doing in this place really, really mattered.

Matt and I wondered what we could and should talk about during that sacred time in those sacred spaces. We revisited parents' needs for raising caring and kind children, and our church's need to de-clutter and simplify our message. Augustine's biblical message of love kept coming back into our conversations, as I lamented that no one ever taught *me* that version. Then the answer seemed perfectly obvious. In those spaces during that time, we would do more of what parents and children need, and more of what the world needs: Love.

• •

It wasn't a search for community that led me to Saint Barnabas. Rather, I suspected that I wouldn't see a single soul from my particular world in the pews and that was the point—I came for the promise of quiet contemplation and, perhaps, anonymity.

In Sunday school, we tell the children that Jesus wants us to love, and care for, and protect everyone. When this is framed in the context of their families, understanding comes quick. When I tell them that this love must include our neighbors and friends, they nod in agreement. It's easy to love those familiar to us, those that look like us. But loving someone we've never met, and probably never will? It can be hard to teach, let alone comprehend.

But because I am, now, a member of the Saint Barnabas community, I know that this isn't a lesson reserved solely for the children. When Matt preaches to us of the people suffering violence and war in Syria, or political rifts that shut down compassionate dialogue, I don't think he's telling us simply to be sympathetic. His weekly reminder of Jesus's call for love and empathy, well, it's the same that we teach our five-year-olds. It turns out that we need to be reminded every step of the way that radical community isn't really that radical of an idea.

I still don't see the faces of my close friends and family when I look around the pews at St. Barnabas. But teaching Sunday school has made the obvious clear to me: Jesus wants us to define a community by more than what is comfortable and familiar. And with pipe cleaners and play-dough, the preschoolers and I are learning that by expanding our notion of community, we grow in love. —Flannery R.

• •

Fortunately, Jesus had some great ideas about love as shown in his teachings, the people he healed, and the marginalized he turns our attention toward. There is no end to how you can talk about love in the Christian context. It's a theme that can go on and on and on and on and on. Jesus seemed to repeat himself a lot, so maybe we should too.

This was not a huge stretch, as far as the Christian tradition goes. It was a leap from what was normally done in children's formation, but not far from what the church says we're supposed to be doing a lot of. Jesus made it clear that to follow God was to show love to one another. If we're no longer proclaiming that message or feel like our children don't understand that, then we have some work to do.

While it may seem I have chosen to redirect our focus from the Bible, it's not the case. The focus of our program on love comes *directly out of the Bible*. This is Augustine's version: the simmered-down version of the Bible, or that precious quart of maple syrup after boiling ten gallons of sap. In either case, it's the best thing to serve children on any given Sunday morning.

Love Self (September–October)

We decided to divide our curriculum into three units: Love Self, Love Neighbor, and Love God, and work in a linear fashion, capitalizing on the flow of the school calendar and secular holidays. As our school year begins, children use the Love Self unit to introduce themselves to our community, highlighting things that they love and what they love about themselves. We intentionally do activities and projects that reinforce that we are all lovable in the eyes of God, and that what makes us unique is where God is at work. Teachers especially focus on qualities or traits that are related to empathy or caring for others, making clear to children that love, kindness, and generosity are highly valued in our community.

Following the Love Self unit of our first year, we had our first children's worship service. In front of the rest of the congregation, children were invited to make and share a decorated poster, highlighting one thing they loved about themselves. Without much guidance from teachers, most children chose to write, "I am loving." While I don't have the metrics to scientifically prove that our program is actually making children value love and kindness, I can say for certain that they know *this* is a place where love and kindness receive high praise and are unanimously welcomed and encouraged. And that's a good start.

Self-care is also part of loving ourselves and caring for the body, mind, and spirit that God has given us. We talk about the importance of eating healthy foods, resting our active minds with yoga or mindfulness, exercising regularly, and spending time outdoors. We also talk about relationships and how these impact our own sense of self. Children discuss what good friends look like, how we like to be treated, who is a member of our family, and how we show love in our families.

We also talk about the feelings we *don't* love as much that are still part of who we are: anger, sadness, anxiety, envy, grief, or fear. We normalize these feelings, letting children know that they are part of being human. We acknowledge these feelings—in ourselves, too—and help children find ways to manage these feelings in productive ways. Children often offer stories about when they were scared or afraid, angry or jealous. Special attention is given to letting children know they are not alone and that there are strategies for dealing with these emotions in ways that don't hurt others.

We talk about how we can sometimes be hard on ourselves and how we can practice giving ourselves positive messages. We offer prayer as a way to communicate with God, using our prayers as a way to further develop empathy for others, but also as a way to calm oneself when emotions are feeling overwhelming. We aim to show children the comfort that prayer can bring.

Love Self was partly in response to many parents' concerns about their children's anxiety, fragile self-esteem, or vulnerability to peer pressure. Parents wanted their children to know that despite not always feeling lovable or perfect, that they *are* loved and they are perfect human beings, flaws and all. I hardly know any adult who *truly* has all the Love of Self that they need; it seems most of us need steady reminders that we are loved, and that we are lovable and worthy. Our children are no different.

When we first brainstormed this portion of the curriculum, it was meant to support parents in their pursuit to raise children who understood they were lovable, that their uniqueness—and quirkiness—is what makes them precious. For some children, these messages are not clear from their parents, making our community all the more important. Our job might not be merely to *reinforce* that children are lovable, but to be the first ones who've ever claimed it was true. One of the assumptions of this program is that all children need love. And they need it first.

Love Neighbor (January–March)

Our second unit is Love Neighbor, the heart of the program, and the practical application of Jesus's greatest teaching: to love our neighbor. With repeated opportunities to serve others, children learn that church is where we commit to love and care for others, and that they are capable of making a difference. Relying heavily on the Good Samaritan and Jesus's greatest commandment to love our neighbor, children are taught that this is the crux of our Christian belief system, and the one that defines us as a community. Large, attractive posters with the Golden Rule are hung in every classroom and in the hallway, signaling that this is what we value in this space.

Children act out the parable of the Good Samaritan in different ways, using puppets or performing skits. Teachers linger with this story for weeks because of the importance it plays in children's lives today; children have loved revisiting this parable week after week. We invite children to create their own versions using scenarios that they've confronted in their everyday lives; they have, and they will tell you. In my experience, this parable is one of the most relatable biblical stories for children. We cannot miss the opportunity to help them verbalize the courage it takes to be the Good Samaritan, the pain of being the one who is ignored, the regularity with which it occurs to us today, and then practice responding to these situations in ways that reflect our core beliefs as Christians.

• •

The Sunday school I went to as a child was not a progressive, nurturing, and inspiring place. When my parents learned that my older brother had his mouth taped shut for asking too many questions, we stopped going to church. Although I've little memory of attending Sunday school, I certainly had reservations at the prospect of putting my own children in a Sunday school program.

Despite my own hesitations, the Sunday school program at Saint Barnabas has proven to be an enriching experience for my boys. The teachers here are focusing on broad and important ideas behind the Scripture that encourage empathy and love of your neighbor. I find the messages my kids take from the program are ones I can get behind wholeheartedly. —Adam R.

• •

The Love Neighbor unit is filled with age-appropriate service projects and activities that give children regular opportunities to serve others in need, in whatever way *they* can. We plan a range of projects that touch on different themes, with an emphasis on tending to people in our congregation who are ill, grieving, suffering, or in need. In some cases, children and teachers pick a project that is especially important to their class or our community. Some projects last one morning, others stretch over a few weeks, but it's certain that any child attending our Sunday school between Christmas and Easter are actively and deliberately acting out of love to serve those in need.

Our program assumes that no one is too young to do God's work to alleviate the suffering of others. Our class of three- and four-year-olds are happy to do their own projects, touching on caring for animals by painting bird houses for our neighborhood feathered friends or making heart ornaments for homebound parishioners. It's not uncommon to hear an adult ask a three-year-old, "What service project were *you* working on this week?" The youngest ones are aware of what's happening in the older classes and have loved being part of the team. Our job is to provide opportunities for them to do the important work that they *already* want to do.

Love God (April–June)
Our final unit is Love God, a culmination of all the work we have done throughout the year to love all that God has created, finding God in

our work, and recognizing our holy experiences as times when God is there. Classrooms are decorated with banners that simply say, "Where is God in this?" reminding us that the reason we gather is deeply rooted in believing that God is—and that God is *love*. Look for love, we say, and you'll find God right there.

Children experience holy things in their lives; they feel love in their relationships and in special moments and in special places. Our program doesn't assume that children are waiting for us to tell them about God. It is quite the opposite. We help children examine the people and places where they find love, looking for God in loving interactions and actions. When they name where love can be found in their lives, we point to what they already know to be holy, telling them that God is there in that loving and holy space. Since Danny was two, he's been ruminating about God, wondering where and why and how it all works. I confess rather easily that I don't know all the answers to his questions. But when he asks where God is, I point to his nose, then slowly point to mine and back to his, and say, "God is right there." That, I know for sure.

Love God is a reflective unit where we revisit much of what we did throughout the year and talk about it more deeply as it relates to God. We revisit prayer and how communicating with God can be useful when life feels overwhelming and days seem difficult. Children are encouraged to pray in ways that resonate with them, whether doodling, journaling, or using prayer beads. We assume that—much like everything else—each child has their own way of finding meaning in prayer and we offer multiple opportunities for children to find one that fits.

We revisit our discussions about gratitude, thanking God for the many blessings in our lives. On the heels of a unit about loving our neighbors in need, children feel more confident about all that they are grateful for.

We talk about people we love who have died, but how our love for them hasn't. Children share what it was like to lose a favorite grandparent or a beloved pet, some recounting stories with great confidence about God's role in it, while some feel confused and unsure. As a gift to these children, we don't shy away from these difficult conversations. Instead, we have readied and prepared the space *for* these difficult conversations. We commit to being honest about what we know—and what we don't—about death. Children learn that God is there whenever love is present, even if we're feeling happy or sad. God is not conditional, but rather accompanies us through the joyful *and* sorrowful times.

• •

In Sunday school I learned that God is love, and you should love your enemies. Before, when I was just five, I thought that bad guys were just *bad*, but now I know that you should love people, even if they're your enemy. One time, when a friend said, "Oh God!" I asked her, "Do you know what that means? God is really Love. I've been learning about it, and it's pretty good!" —Sam R.

• •

Holidays
This format has built-in transitions marking the end of each unit, naturally making space for the non-sectarian and Christian holidays that are such a big part of our culture. In November and as Thanksgiving approaches, we focus on gratitude and giving, particularly what we are grateful for in our lives and what gifts of love we have to give. We spend the month of December talking about the story of Jesus's birth, and how this intersects with our Christmas customs and traditions. I once overheard Sam, our six-year-old, matter-of-factly telling Millie, "Santa brings us presents because Jesus died," signaling that there's some real confusion among children about Jesus and Santa Claus, who came first, and how one is related to the other. We try to help children make sense of these intertwined traditions, so they have a fuller understanding of how their Christian tradition relates to these holidays.

The Love Neighbor unit naturally ends around Lent when we shift our focus to the Easter story, how that relates to Jesus's message of loving our neighbors and to the unit to come: Love God. The Easter season and all its mystery prime the children for the mystery that surrounds God, preparing them to think about the complicated parts of our sacred story. As with the rest of the curriculum, when it comes to Christmas and Easter, we highlight the message rooted in love.

• •

CHAPTER 6

Our Gifts

The custom of giving and receiving is so commonplace in our culture that we hardly know it's happening. If you're invited to a friend's house for dinner, you instinctively ask what you can bring. If your child goes to a birthday party, you wouldn't dream of sending them empty-handed. In turn, the hosts are planning what to give *you*, whether it's a prized dessert at dinner, or a party-favor bag—in most cases, there's a gift in return coming your way. I really love this part of American culture. I get it, I understand it, and I participate wholeheartedly in it.

At times, and mostly in cultures new to me, I've taken this natural custom for granted. I mistakenly assumed gift giving was the same everywhere, or that I could pick it up rather quickly. I was a Peace Corps volunteer in Cameroon, and during that time I made my fair share of mistakes. I now understand that polishing your shoes despite living on a dirt road in the rainy season shows respect for the person you're going to meet, or building an outdoor kitchen at the bottom of a hill during the dry season means it'll be gone on the first day of the rainy season. But the gift giving, I almost always got incorrect.

All of my Cameroonian neighbors cooked in outdoor kitchens with cast-iron pots blazing over roaring fires. And all of these women would lift their cast-iron pots off the fire with their *bare hands*. Some of the younger neighbors might use a scrap piece of paper to protect their hands, but most wouldn't. This was almost unbearable to watch, and

I spent the first few months gasping aloud each time I saw it. It motivated me to take a bus to the capital, call my mom, and ask for her help to fix this problem. "Mom, we're in desperate need of potholders. Please send some!" When the potholders finally arrived, I was bubbling over with excitement and promptly walked the neighborhood distributing these gems like they were the hand-saving tools that they *definitely* were. As expected, everyone was thrilled to receive such a beautiful gift from America. And *I* was thrilled to be on my way to changing the world, just like I'd hoped to do in these two years. It was happening, I could tell.

A month later, I visited one of the recipients of the potholders. She excitedly ushered me into her living room and gave me the seat facing one of her drab cement walls. And in the middle of that wall was a three-inch nail; hanging on the nail was my American potholder. I had such mixed emotions, feeling completely embarrassed for giving such a dumb gift, but also feeling really impressed with my neighbor's ingenuity; the potholder *really* dressed up her wall. Fifteen years later, I'm not sure if it's still hanging on the cement wall. But I'm certain of one thing: it was never used as a potholder.

I didn't like it when my Cameroonian friends, neighbors, and colleagues misunderstood my gifts. So much effort, so little reward. When my time in Cameroon was done, I wasn't disappointed to return to a place I better understood.

More than a decade later, though, I'm wondering if perhaps those gifts were not the disasters I'd feared. My potholder gift most definitely *wasn't* a protective covering for fingertips, like I'd intended; that much was obvious. But oddly enough my neighbors still thought it was a gift. So then maybe my gift to give—in the end—was not a potholder, but *friendship*. I asked my mother to ship something across the world for my neighbors, and it was this gesture of kindness that my friends needed most. Without knowing it, that was the gift I had to give.

On any given Sunday morning, you never know what gifts people will receive, whether it is the music, the silence or stillness, the fellowship. Nor do we know what gifts people will give: teaching, serving, or friendship. We only know that there are many to be given.

Our Gifts to Children

Children are not merely objects to be ministered to or young under-developed Christians awaiting maturity. Nor are they simply a safe-guard against the decline of the church. On the contrary, children are valuable to the life of any congregation in a real and authentic way. Churches should always be thinking of what gifts it offers children in return for the gifts they bring. One of the greatest gifts we can give children is to recognize them as full members of the church, and then commit to treating them that way.

Children as full members of the church means doing what it takes to make that happen, but it also means believing that *it's true*. It means caring for their spaces, but also believing that they're sacred. It means affirming their feelings, not only because they really need us to do that but also because we believe their feelings and experiences *are* full and meaningful and sometimes difficult to comprehend. It also means listening to their ideas, not only because we're patient and kind people but also because their ideas are unique and inspiring, and unlike any approach an adult would take. Whether big or small, rich or poor, rural or urban, thriving children's program or not, every church has something to give to children. Loving adults, safe spaces, meaningful conversations, support and encouragement—these are all invaluable gifts that we have to offer children that we should give as freely and as willingly as possible.

Our program makes a conscious effort to dip into the vat of gifts and talents from others in the congregation. Not everyone feels called to be a teacher, so we make room for people who feel called to support our children in other ways. We've found that the unlikeliest volunteers are sometimes the best, offering gifts we didn't know we needed or they weren't sure they had. Regardless of the person or the gift, any additional loving adult that joins the children on a Sunday morning is giving a gift to children. The more adults that are part of the children's ministry, the more the children will believe—and know—that they are important to the life of the parish, and that other adults in our Christian community care about them.

Your Gifts

When it comes to a Sunday school program, there are very few people who feel they have the right gifts to be a teacher. Even our *actual* teachers sometimes question being at the helm of children's religious education. One of our teachers, Flannery, often confesses, "I don't think I know enough about this to be teaching it." As I was recruiting our teachers earlier that year, this insecurity was always on my mind. The assumption of our program, Love First, is that *everyone* has a gift to give the children in our church. It merely takes some creativity and openness about what those gifts are and how they fit into our program. If you have patience, please come sit with us. If you love to plant flowers, please come plant with us. If you have a favorite book, please come read it to us. If you care deeply about an organization that helps others in need, please come tell us about it.

Months before I asked for volunteers, I wrote an article in our church newsletter about rethinking Sunday school and how adults might incorporate their special gifts into the children's program. I received a lot of feedback from that article. Mostly, though, people were totally confused. One woman said to me, "I'm not sure how someone's talent for baking bread is relevant to Sunday school, but I'm curious to see where this is going!"

For children, it seems obvious that we love the gifts they bring, and we impose no such restrictions or requirements on their gifts. Come as you are, we say. *You* are the gift. Children are naturally energetic, enthusiastic, and full of wonder. They aren't afraid to ask difficult questions, unknowingly sparking conversations that are complicated and enriching, and not often started by self-conscious adults. Children make us laugh, not only because they're funny, because they remind us of what we might look like without the baggage we've accumulated along the way. Without even trying, children are valuable assets to any family and to any community, and what they have to offer is almost impossible to replicate without them.

But that's true for adults, too. Come as you are. *You* are the gift to our children, I say. I am eager for adults to come into our classrooms because their presence speaks volumes about the importance of children to the life of our church. The more adults who visit our spaces and get to know our children, the more connected children feel when they walk into the church. This also leaves others feeling proud of the gifts they *do* have, builds relationships, and strengthens our Christian community as a whole. So, yes, baking bread or making worm farms together is important to our church community, and essential to creating the kind of children's ministry that impacts the whole church.

Adults, too, stand to gain quite a bit by coming into our classrooms and offering their gifts. They are not only *giving* of themselves, they are *receiving* gifts—sometimes unexpectedly. For some of our volunteers, they received gifts that they didn't know they wanted or needed. And on our best days, working with the children has changed volunteers' entire experience at church: deepening the depth and widening the breadth of their connectedness to our entire community.

The Big Ask

My mom loves to tell the story about the day I turned two years old. As she remembers it, I was completely agreeable for the first two years of my life. And then—out of nowhere—I couldn't handle being told "no," and haven't changed a bit. To hear her tell the story, it's clear she *really* enjoyed the first two years of my life.

Lucky for her, this job is finally getting me used to hearing "no."

Recruiting teachers is no easy task for the person in charge of getting volunteers for a children's program, or any program for that matter. If you've ever had to do this, you already know it comes with a ton of rejection and possibly some demoralization. And even after volunteers accept, the stress lingers knowing they can quit at any moment. I've lost more sleep over worrying about teachers than any other aspect of designing and implementing a children's program. It is—without a doubt—the most challenging part of this job for me. Regardless of your curriculum or your space or your church, *teachers* are the loving adults who are ultimately responsible for shaping the time and space for the children in our presence. Great programs must have great teachers. And judging by everyone's reluctance to commit, I think that must be obvious.

Two months into this job, when I was still deliberating whether to commit to the following year, we celebrated the end of our Sunday school year. Our rector at the time, Patti, wanted to thank *all* the adults who had volunteered with the children over the past year. With every volunteer standing to applause, there were a total of five. *Five* adults had volunteered in the classrooms that year. Five. Total. In a church of three hundred, that simply won't do.

Five minutes later, and always up for a challenge, I decided to take the job, and immediately set out to build my children's ministry team. At the next year's celebration when volunteers were asked to stand up, I imagined more than five (*way* more than five). I'd envisioned doing great things in the upcoming year with our wonderful children, and I wanted more than five people to be part of it.

Prior to making a single request to potential volunteers, I talked to a half-dozen *other* people (clergy, administrators, committee heads) about adults they thought might be a good match for the children's ministry: someone who would be interested, qualified, or simply looking for a place to fit in or connect to the church community. This list was a cinch to generate. In no time, I had a list of twenty-seven names—some I knew and some I didn't—scribbled on the back of a used envelope with tons of notes, circled and crossed-out names, jotted down phone numbers or e-mail addresses. For the entire summer, I guarded this envelope with my life.

Looking at this long list of names, it was clear that I didn't need everyone to be a teacher; I only needed three to say yes, leaving a whopping twenty-four people completely off the hook. Those odds were pretty good, I thought. The thing is, I'd heard really good arguments for why *all* twenty-seven people would be a good match for the children's ministry. And despite not feeling like I needed them, I wanted them all.

I never sent a single mass e-mail looking for volunteers; that method is not only unproductive, it's *counter*productive. Rarely does it result in a volunteer, and mass e-mails are far too easy for loads of people to ignore, often leaving the requestor feeling discouraged or even unsupported. Mass e-mail requests for volunteers are only efficient if you want to get as many rejections as possible in the shortest amount of time. Consider a different approach, one that involves ministering to people to learn about what they love to do and what they might want to share with the children. Assume the people in your congregation *want* to support the work of the children, and then find a way to make it happen in a way that has a positive impact on the children *and* this reticent volunteer. In other words, love first.

When I began writing to or approaching people about volunteering, I gave as much information as possible about what I was trying to do, how I thought they would fit, *and* what other opportunities were available if the weekly commitment didn't suit them. These e-mails or conversations were long and personal, and well worth the time spent— these were not merely requests, but a way for me to share the vision of my program with twenty-seven new people *and*—if I'm being honest—to keep from hearing the dreaded "no." Perhaps I haven't changed much at all since my second birthday.

I did get a handful of rejections; some people were moving or working and were literally unable to be there on Sundays. But mostly, I got a whole lot of "no, but . . .," which—for the first time in my life—was music to my ears. People were interested in participating and supporting the program, but wanted something other than the pressure or commitment of being a lead teacher. Each person honestly told me how much time they could offer: an hour a month, an hour a year, Wednesday morning, babysitting while I did the youth group (seriously, I got free babysitting out of some of my requests). It turns out nearly everyone wanted to participate in unconventional ways, sharing their time and talent in ways I hadn't even thought of. They had the *best* ideas: a retired speech therapist wanted to teach the youngest children a song in sign language; an avid gardener wanted to plant flowers on Earth Day; a crafter wanted to prepare art projects on a weekday morning. And some wanted to sit with wiggly kids during a messy project, join us for yoga, or teach the kids how to be lectors or ushers.

I'd never been so happy to hear the word "no." But even so, I was much, *much* happier when three said "yes." And at our end-of-the-year celebration that year we thanked thirty-three volunteers.

Teachers

One of the reasons so many people shy away from teaching Sunday school is that it sounds like an absurdly large task. Someone once said to me, "I don't know how you do it. I could *never* be in charge of any-one's *entire* religious education." Had I realized that's what people expected of me, I'd never have agreed to teach Sunday school in the first place, because how is that *one person's* job? The main reason for people's reluctance to sign on: no one felt qualified. Watching Flannery struggle with whether or not she was good at this made me realize that somewhere someone gave the wrong impression that we needed highly skilled scholars to teach Sunday school. We don't need that. And, in fact, we don't *want* that. There's no reason why someone like Flannery should feel out of place as a teacher. She is kind, patient, compassionate, and humble; she is *everything* we want in a teacher.

We can't claim to know it all—and we shouldn't want only teachers who feel comfortable doing so. Not only would that be false, it would be unhelpful to children if they think adults have all the answers. We are meant to be loving people who encourage them to love, to care for others, and to find God in their work and in their lives. If there are things that we're still learning it's important to let the children know, foreshadowing a future that might get complicated and confusing one day. There's room for uncertainty in this place. Church isn't always the place where you go to find the answers; it can be where you go and with whom you surround yourself while you *try* to find them. Most adults with mature faith know there aren't always answers, but we keep coming back, finding comfort in the journey.

• •

Love First taught me that my role as a Sunday school teacher was not to grow children into theologians. My role was to inspire children to use the gifts that God has given them to minister to their church and to their community. Not only was that a lot less intimidating, but empowering. Teaching children to minister to their neighbors helped to simplify my own perception of faith. I have learned that being a devoted Christian is not just memorizing the Scripture and going to church every Sunday. It's about realizing the gifts that God has given you and using those gifts to the benefit of those around you.

I have not only experienced how this model can transform a church and even a community; I have felt it transform *me*, into a leader in children's ministries. I never imagined I would I have that title, but I now know it's what God meant for me. —Katie B.

• •

Our teachers are not theologians and never set out to be. Matt has been studying the doctrines of the church for decades and is still working on it, so I can only assume that it takes considerably more time than we have on a Sunday morning. What children need is someone exactly like Flannery who is always happy to see them on Sunday mornings, and who feels like being with them is as real as church gets for her.

Teacher Commitment = More Opportunity

Originally, I proposed the team-teaching approach as a way to relieve the burden of commitment when trying to get volunteers in classrooms. I mistakenly assumed that this would encourage more people to sign on, but it did little to assuage the time commitment for them. Even so, when I offered this option to the teachers who *had* accepted, they all declined the team-teaching model and instead preferred to come every week. They were less interested in handing the class off to another person for half of the month, preferring instead to feel more connected to the children by knowing what happened from week to week.

For us, this has been crucial to creating a safe place for children to gather. Seeing a familiar face when children walk into the room helps parents prepare their children for the morning, and also provides constancy and consistency that is essential to the work we're trying to do. Just like having a different pastor or priest every Sunday might get in the way of the ritual or routine, the same is true for Sunday school. The teachers are part of the children's routine and part of the classroom rituals. Additionally, when teachers develop close connections to children, they are better equipped to minister to them. And children are more willing to share what's important to them, making the gatherings more meaningful.

Do More, Get More

The first year of Love First, I planned every lesson and every activity for every class every Sunday of the year. I did it for two reasons: 1) I promised teachers I would, in exchange for their commitment to teach, and 2) the program wasn't done yet. It was still taking shape in our living room after the kids went to bed, changing and molding to the families in front of us. If it looked like children needed something different, we made a change for the following week because we'd committed to tending to their needs. I couldn't expect teachers to sit on our couch with Matt and me every evening, so it made the most sense to write the lesson plans for them.

• •

I believe in grounding my children in values of caring, pride, empathy, hope, faith, self-worth, and love.

This approach to teaching children about religion has been freeing, non-confining and relatable. To see a group of children transform into a compassionate, caring, reflective group of friends has given me overwhelming joy, and it has enriched my life. Love First, for me, is about grounding our children in God's love, and helping them recognize that that love exists in all parts of their lives. I see God in my classroom. I feel God in our circle time. And I witness God's love when I see the love that children have for one another.

Love First allows me to listen to the needs of the children in front of me, customize, change, and develop each week with careful thought. How will this lesson impact how they feel about themselves? How will it build empathy towards others? How will it help them feel connected to God? My goal was to make our Sunday school class a desirable, exciting and rewarding time in our children's week. The bigger gain, though, has been having my children grow up to be compassionate, caring adults who recognize the beauty life brings, knowing God is by their side. — Jackie D.

• •

Halfway through our Love Neighbor unit, teachers hit their stride. They knew the routine, the children, and the expectations of the program. And they were itching to do certain things with their class, particularly as it related to loving their neighbor. Our last service project for Love Neighbor was still up in the air, so I invited teachers to choose a project or cause that was meaningful to them. I don't think I was done getting those words out of my mouth before all three teachers told me their plan: Flannery wanted to talk about refugees, Bette about vermiculture, and Jackie about disabilities. All they needed from me was permission to run with their ideas. It shouldn't come as a surprise that these were among the best-planned classes of the year: teachers using their own gifts, talents, and expertise combined with interests of the children in their class to plan lessons that were meaningful to everyone. Our curriculum invites everyone to think of their gifts as opportunities to breathe life into our children's program and into our congregation, and it looked like teachers were finally starting to believe it.

When I learned that all of the teachers would be returning the following year, I used the money that would normally be spent on purchasing a curriculum, and instead offered it to the teachers to participate in a daylong workshop. Together, we spent an entire day discussing the highlights and drawbacks of the year, what should be modified, added, or tossed. I gave guidelines for themes and biblical stories that must be covered for the following year and a rhythm for the flow of the morning, but otherwise I invited teachers to find books, stories, activities, and projects that suited their interests, teaching style, and the children in their class.

And they did—with great enthusiasm. The following year, teachers were more excited about what they were teaching, and they felt more prepared. They were more invested in the program, in their class, and the children in front of them. Teaching is *their* ministry, after all, and my job was less about making it easy for them, and more about empowering them to use their gifts to make it a meaningful experience.

The Gift of Mentoring

Whenever we have an upcoming children's worship service (see chapter 8), I invite regular ushers and lectors to help the children learn more about these roles and get them prepared to perform them at the service. This has been such a fun and easy way to incorporate adults into the children's program, and everyone enjoys it. I used to stick to asking people who have a known interest in working with children, tending toward the group of loving retired grandmothers (of which we have plenty at Saint Barnabas).

On the morning of one of our children's services, there was a scheduling mix-up, and Frank, one of our regular ushers, was scheduled to work with the children. He was nervous about it, but was second in command behind Lois, who was a former Sunday school teacher and had previously helped the children usher. Lois whispered to me, "Frank's really nervous and isn't sure how he'll do. I told him, 'It's actually fun. You'll do fine, Frank.'"

Twenty minutes later, I noticed Frank leading our children down the aisle, carefully going through the motions of being an usher, taking every opportunity to tell each child about the sacred elements, and how to handle and carry them. While helping a little girl, Addison, dismiss pews, I overheard Frank saying to each row of people, "This is *Addi*, she'll be your usher today."

• •

When I was asked to help teach children the customary ushering role, as a fairly new usher myself, I initially felt unsure. I wanted to be helpful to the growing number of children in our program who were also seamlessly being integrated into our church community, now becoming truly visible and a noticeable presence.

Lois and I put on our name tags, introduced ourselves, and talked about our experiences being ushers and how we felt about the tasks we were there to do. Answering the children's questions, it became clear to me that this experience was also a great opportunity for me to refresh my own approaches as an usher. I needed to consider how to see this experience as the children see it, through fresh eyes.

We realized how important it was for us to be mindful and respectful of the children's innocence as well as the anxiety they were probably experiencing. We needed to allow them their natural and raw excitement and eagerness to please, and we did not want to inhibit their enthusiasm. And we wanted them to trust and be comfortable with us.

I had a blast with the children. The children's innocence mixed with their energy brought out my desire to be the best usher I could be with them.

The overall usher experience for me, and I believe for the children, was a shared experience of grace and a reminder of the essence of community worship. Through the innocence of children we were able to go about doing brave things that day, as well as honoring age-old traditions.
—Frank G.

• •

The kids loved this. They giggled together throughout the service as Frank guided them along. And they giggled afterwards while retelling stories about Frank, especially when he welcomed visitors entering the church by asking, "Do you want a program from *me*, or from one of these lovely young ladies?"

Frank's enthusiasm for his role as usher was a gift to our children. He not only shared part of himself with our children, but a role in our church usually reserved for adults. And as it turned out, he loved it too (which was totally obvious). At Frank's request, he has helped with every children's worship service since. And kids are drawing straws to get to usher with Frank.

Unexpected Gifts

One of our teachers, Bette, taught me a lot about the limited ways we were letting people support our children's ministry. Because Bette is a kind and caring team player, she agreed to teach one of the classes despite not feeling like it was one of her gifts. She believed in the program and wanted to be supportive, so I was eager to add her to the teaching team. As the first year rolled on, it became clear that teaching was not Bette's ministry. Despite my pep talks, she politely and patiently told me she would agree to continue just so long as I agreed to look for a replacement.

I accepted her pending resignation.

When I found a replacement, I asked Bette if there was any way she'd like to continue to be part of the program to preserve her connection to the kids. She hesitated a bit and said with some trepidation, "Well, what do you think about *worm farms*?" I think about worm farms how I feel about baking bread—we can make that work. And so Bette was replaced, and returned as a guest volunteer to work on a three-week vermiculture unit with her former class. After the first vermiculture class, her replacement, Katie, remarked, "Bette was on fire, Colette. She was totally in her element."

Bette is no longer the teacher who felt like she didn't have the right gifts to give. Instead, she's the scientist losing sleep over climate change who shared with the kids something that was of importance to her: a creative and important way to love the Earth and our neighbors. And now we have Katie, who actually feels like teaching is *her* ministry. A win-win.

The Gift of Stories

We have a tradition at Saint Barnabas of inviting long-time members into the classrooms for a panel discussion. I loved the intention behind this, and wanted to continue to honor this long-time tradition. Instead of surprising the children with these visits, though, we planned carefully in the previous weeks. Teachers and children discussed the importance of listening to others, the value of elders' stories, and then brainstormed questions that were meaningful to the children, in hopes of our elder guests learning more about what's important to the children. I opted for two individuals instead of a group to make it a more intimate experience, and I chose two people I'd known to be the kind and loving people who children should get to know better.

When our guests arrived, the children filed into Jackie's rug room, placing themselves on the floor with note cards in hand while our guests, Dick and Cynthia, sat on the comfy chairs in front of them. It was a lovely half hour of sharing stories, Dick reminiscing about what the church grounds looked like when he was a kid more than eighty years ago, Cynthia responding to a question about where she finds God. Dick shared a story about how his older brother, Bob, passed up a chance to go to Harvard, opting instead for a more affordable option so the family could send Dick to college, too. Dick shared with the children how selfless his brother had been, and how fortunate he was—both to go to college *and* to have a big brother who was so generous toward him. Dick's retelling of this story was one of love, sacrifice, and generosity. It was clear that although it happened seventy-some years ago, it was still very important to Dick and something he wanted to share with the children.

As we were winding down, a seven-year-old girl of mixed race asked Cynthia, who is African American, "Have you ever been judged by the color of your skin?" Cynthia grew quiet for a moment and thoughtfully responded, "Yes. I *have* been judged by the color of my skin, and it makes me *so mad.*" She shared with the children how she used to react as a child when others judged her by her skin and how she responds now as an older woman, subtly letting children know that it has happened all her life. When Cynthia finished, she looked at the children staring back at her and told them, "You all give me hope that this world will become a better place."

In these moments, Cynthia's and Dick's stories were their gifts to these children sitting before them. They became real people before our very eyes, people we came to care deeply about in only thirty minutes time. If either of these loving adults hadn't walked into these classrooms because they didn't feel called to be a teacher, the children would've missed this valuable opportunity to connect to two very loving adults— and in fact, Cynthia and Dick would've missed out too. These opportunities are everywhere in a church. Sure, people have special talents and interests worth sharing, but sometimes it's honest stories that are gift enough.

Staff

I would be remiss if I didn't touch on the importance of working with staff, whether volunteer or paid. In most cases, they are a huge part of the behind-the-children's-ministry scene. Their commitment to the program is crucial to its success, and using *their* gifts will make your children's ministry stronger and more meaningful to the whole church. Clergy are a valuable resource for addressing theological questions that inevitably come from children, parents, and teachers. I can't pretend to be a theologian; the only reason it was possible to develop a theologically sound program that also matched the overall vision of our church was that I worked with the clergy (one of whom happens to be my spouse). In addition to developing a curriculum together, I regularly seek Matt's counsel or advice on how best to present things to children like baptism, Palm Sunday, or the Resurrection. If something is confusing to me, I assume it might be equally confusing to our teachers as well as the children.

It also means working closely with your church administrator, who knows—probably better than anyone—what's happening, who's doing it, and how to get things done. Our administrator, Margaret, has daily contact with members, so it is a benefit to the children's ministry to keep her abreast of what we're doing. The sextons are the people who lovingly prepare the building to receive children on Sunday mornings; their help is crucial to maintaining sacred spaces and welcoming families onto our campus. Our music ministry is a complementary ministry to our children's program and is indispensable when planning children's special worship services. Our music director, Deb, always knows the perfect song to teach the children at any given time of year and I happily utilize her expertise.

Parents' Gifts

Perhaps even *more* important than realizing that everyone brings their own gifts to church, is realizing that sometimes people don't bring the gifts you expect them to bring. I thought I'd learned that lesson with Bette, or even the potholders, but I guess there was more to learn. Our church-wide volunteer base is largely made up of retirees—not *just* the young-ish sixty-five-year-old ones, but the seventy-, eighty-, and even ninety-year-olds. Our major events and ministries are run on the sweat and energy of aging parishioners who dedicate a great deal of time to Saint Barnabas. They are tremendous and overworked human beings. Many have asked me, "Why can't the young families do this? We're tired."

I usually respond, "We are too. Can you give us a few years?"

A generation or two ago, church—and life—often looked a lot different: men usually worked, women typically stayed home with children. And church reflected this dynamic by having committees comprised mostly of men while women stayed home and watched the children. Today, Saint Barnabas barely resembles the church of those days of old. With single parents, dual working parents, mothers becoming the primary breadwinner, and committees led by men *and* women, families—and how they come to church—look a lot different.

It often goes unmentioned—though I hope not unnoticed—that the majority of young families coming to church are mothers and children. In the first two years of our Love First program, we welcomed twenty new families, sixteen of which were single parents in the pews. Typically one parent—and almost always the mother—came to church with the children, and the other parent—almost always the father—stayed home. Men's attendance at church has steadily declined over the years, which means that families have to choose whether to be together or apart on Sunday mornings, *and* that this group of mostly women are being asked to fill volunteer roles while still being responsible for children. Most churches haven't realized this yet, and thus haven't adequately tended to the unique demands that this dynamic presents.

Either way, this is affecting how churches function, particularly whether or not they are able to be welcoming to parents and whether the aging volunteers can get some reprieve. If churches *really* want to tend to children and families as well as the older folks who need a rest from their volunteer positions, they must recognize the needs of the young families in front of them. A mother with two toddlers is not an ideal volunteer if she has to watch her children while doing it. Additionally, a household with two working parents who rarely see each other means Saturday workdays or leadership retreats for one committed parent can really throw off an entire household.

At Saint Barnabas, we've found two things to be essential: making it meaningful and offering child care. Anyone running a meeting should consider time with parents as precious and think carefully about what happens during *that* precious hour. Use it wisely, make it consequential, and acknowledge it might have been difficult for parents to get there and that their time is valuable. When young parents are asked to volunteer, pay attention to who you are asking: is it a parent who often comes alone? If so, consider if they would or *could* volunteer with children. If volunteering at church means finding costly child care, it might not be a wise financial move for parents to volunteer despite their desire to help. If their presence and participation is important, find a way to make it not only possible—but enjoyable—for them. At Saint Barnabas, we are doing our best to pay attention to the parents in our midst to determine if they're there to serve, or to *be* served. It makes a difference. And the whole church depends upon it.

The Gifts of the Whole Church

When Millie was two, Matt and I started thinking about taking her to Sunday school. In preparation for the big day, I perused the hallways of our children's program—for the first time ever—and was struck by the separation from the rest of the church, both physically and spiritually. It was Sunday morning, and children and teachers were busily scurrying around in one part of the church campus, while "real church" was happening on the other side of the campus, simultaneously occurring but without any noticeable integration or connection. Halfway through the service during the peace, a group of children would tiptoe into the back of the church and reunite with parents in the back few rows while the church service seamlessly carried on.

This lack of integration with the rest of the congregation didn't make sense to me, which meant trying to find *new* ways for the children to be in the church and *new* ways for others to be in the classrooms. To imagine that no one else has anything to offer the children's program is a huge mistake. I didn't want our children's program—and thus the children—to be and feel so separate from the rest of the church. If I noticed it, the children probably did too.

Here's the best news, though: this is not just good for children; it's good for everyone. Instead of having a children's program that reminds people of what they're *not* capable of doing, we have one that reminds them of what they *are* good at doing, of what gifts they have to offer. One of the best—and most surprising—parts of our program is the people who *don't* feel called to be teachers: it's Barbara, the ninety-year-old woman who writes back to a child after receiving a card; Frank, the committed usher who values his role and wants to teach others how to do it; Merrily, the beachcomber who wants to gather shells for children's projects. We don't actually *need* everyone to be a teacher. We just want others to share their gifts. Because the more faces that are recognizable to the children when they enter the church, the more children are recognizable to others. And the more everyone feels like they're an important part of the community, the more it'll feel like home.

CHAPTER 7

Our Ministers

As priest's kids, our children get a lot of attention at Saint Barnabas. When Millie was a few weeks old, a gentleman rushed up to me at coffee hour and said, "You know, she's really the *church's* baby." The scene of the labor still fresh in my mind, I told him that I didn't recall the church being there for the delivery. So, no, she wasn't the church's at all. She was, in fact, all mine.

However, by the time our third child, Danny, arrived on the scene, I was much more willing to share the wealth and grew to enjoy the outpouring of love and attention we got on Sunday mornings. We don't live anywhere near our extended family, which—I'm certain—was only bearable because of the love that Saint Barnabas showered upon us. It was great. And I became a *huge* fan of church. When I got to know other young families at Saint Barnabas, it was clear that this adulation and affection was reserved for our family mostly. In other words, no one ever claimed that *other* people's children belonged to the church.

It makes sense how this happened, and why churches think babies of clergy belong to them (actually, that part is still weird). Everyone in church already felt connected to Matt. He invites others into our life by sharing our family's stories from the pulpit, he participates in their most joyful celebrations and their most sorrowful losses; he is part of their lives in real and meaningful ways. So I understand why parishioners would reciprocate a feeling of love and closeness for his family.

I'd been warned by other priests' wives and preachers' kids that this would feel suffocating, that it would feel like too much for me, but I have never found that to be true.

I grew to know these people as devoted and loving surrogate grandparents who had so, so much love to give. I only wondered why it wasn't being spread around to other families. The other children were lovable, and these pseudo-grandparents weren't choosy about love. I wondered if it *wasn't* a lack of love surrounding these individuals, but that the love just didn't know where to go. And if there were a way to connect these loving adults and lovable children in an authentic way, maybe the love would begin to point toward each other.

Spreading the Love

I took this job shortly after Easter with very little notice or time to prepare. Our program had dwindled to nine regularly attending children and I was the only teacher left. I know some churches can make a one-room schoolhouse style work well, but it's not a comfortable place for me, pedagogically speaking. My head spins trying to think of an activity or story or project (or anything, really) that is engaging enough for ten-year-olds while simple enough for three-year-olds.

One Sunday morning, our multi-age activity was simply to spread love in a way that this span of ages could feel good about. On this particular sunny day, we were going to do this by writing notes and leaving them on parishioners' windshields. Our notes would simply say, "Someone at Saint Barnabas loves you."

The children love, love, *loved* this activity. Some children decorated as many cards as they possibly could, churning them out like a well-run assembly line. Others worked carefully on one or two, knowing exactly which cars would get their cards. Before reuniting with parents in the church, we headed to the parking lot to leave our notes on as many cars as we had cards, children giddy about the secret messages they were leaving for grown-ups.

After church, walking through the parking lot, I noticed a couple get into their car, and then get back out to grab the note from their windshield. The older gentleman, someone I didn't even recognize, read it, smiled, and passed it to the woman seated next to him, who also smiled and tucked the note into her purse. I received several notes and e-mails in the following days from those who found that the notes made them smile; for some it lifted their painfully low spirits. And for one, it felt like a message from God, the exact message of love she needed on a particularly rough day.

When we started the activity, it had been to spread love to others, to let adults know what we were doing in Sunday school. And as expected, it did exactly that. I hadn't anticipated, though, how much joy and satisfaction it would bring the children, knowing they were doing something that might make someone else feel loved. I was convinced that children had an incredible amount of power to spread love in meaningful and authentic ways, and I set out to find as many ways as possible for them to do it.

Soon after, I invited myself to a pastoral care meeting. This ministry is one of our most successful at Saint Barnabas. Our former rector, Patti, pulled together a group of parishioners to do regular pastoral care visits with members no longer able to come to church due to a variety of disabilities. Some of these individuals have physical limitations that keep them homebound, while others are suffering from dementia or other mental limitations. In any case, the reason someone is on the visiting list is because they were once well enough to come to church, and now they aren't. For some, their only connection to church is the regular visits from one of our pastoral care ministers.

These homebound folks are some of our most vulnerable that could benefit most from the love that the children are capable of spreading. This could also help them feel connected to Saint Barnabas in a new way instead of simply feeling the loss of previous connections. I wasn't exactly sure of *everything* the children could offer, but I knew they could make cards. I asked the pastoral care team if forging this connection would be worthwhile, and if we could incorporate this gesture into our children's ministry. Not surprising, the visiting team was enthusiastic about having children send cards, and they sent me on my way with a long, thorough, and updated address list of those who should receive one.

The first year of Love First, children started their morning together making and sending cards to those on the pastoral care list, and we made our way through the names in a few short weeks. The growth of our new program coupled with the industriousness and determination of the children meant we were able to get cards out to many *others* as well. We started sending cards to people who celebrated big birthdays, had surgery, lost a loved one, had a baby, were new to church, or were just lonely and in need of a loving message. Older children wrote letters while younger children decorated cards. Every child was able to send at least one card to someone from the congregation by the end of September.

The response to the children's cards was overwhelming. Some wanted to know how they could or should respond, ready to point the love in the children's direction. I encouraged them to write back—and they did! Children started receiving mail from those they'd written a few weeks earlier, some with detailed instructions about how and where to find them in church (e.g., fourth pew on the left, in front of the pulpit). Children and parents read the notes together and then made their way over to greet the individual during church or coffee hour.

Barbara, a ninety-year-old parishioner who sits in the fourth pew on the left, behind the pulpit, received a card from Caroline, a second grader. Barbara wrote back inviting Caroline to meet her on a Sunday morning, and the two hit it off immediately. Coincidentally, Caroline usually sat in the row directly behind Barbara, so they now happily greet each other every Sunday morning.

• •

Our first years at Saint Barnabas we sat mid-back, and our only awareness of children was hearing youngsters behind us—or seeing a handful coming in the back.

This past year, a new chapter dramatically unfolded.

Beginning in the fall, mid-service, a long procession of children came in the front door, eager to find parents. It soon became a highlight. For health reasons, we now sit very close to the front and can hear the children arriving happily outside. Soon after, we began to receive artwork in the mail with the donor's name.

At the Annual Meeting, Colette suggested the children would love thank-you notes. A very talented young girl, Caroline, received our

notes, in which we had told her where we sit. Very soon we met each other—and she continues to give us lovely artwork. Now each Sunday we look for Caroline, and we greet each other. I was very touched recently when she inquired thoughtfully about my week. We now watch for her and feel she has enriched our Sunday morning. The feeling of being in a church community with Caroline and her family is a blessing. The children's program has truly enriched our Saint Barnabas life.
—Barbara M.

• •

I was visiting Caroline's classroom one morning and invited the class to send cards to a handful of individuals who were in particular need of messages of love. The class immediately set out, writing, decorating, and addressing cards. One child whose loved one recently died of cancer chose to write to someone who was recently diagnosed. Another whose father is an obstetrician decided to write to a retired midwife. All of the children were busy writing to people who they felt connected to by learning about why they were on our list.

Except Caroline. Instead, she worked on a picture of an Easter basket with brightly colored eggs inside. I remember noticing this was unusual for her; most days Caroline prides herself on following directions and sticking to the task. Having forgotten all about it when we headed into the church following Sunday school, I noticed Caroline stop at the fourth pew on the left, right behind the pulpit and hand her Easter drawing to Barbara, who immediately lit up then leaned over to show it to her husband, Tom. They both looked up at her and said, "Thank you, Caroline." She smiled back at them and found her seat.

If Caroline isn't a minister in this church, I don't know who is.

Barbara's experience at Saint Barnabas has been deeply impacted by Caroline, who routinely brings in projects to share with her. Caroline's little sister, Lauren, also offers some of her projects to Barbara or Tom when she comes into church, as if she too wants to be part of the growing love between Caroline and Barbara.

There is no end to this kind of love that sits in our pews on any given Sunday morning waiting to be shared. It is most certainly in the obvious places, but also in the places less obvious, or even unlikely. The important thing to know is that it's there, just waiting to be shared. It might just need a little nudge.

Children as Ministers

One of the core principles of our program is that children can alleviate the suffering of others. They can, and they do. If you've ever felt down, you know a cheesy grin from a three-year-old can really make your heart sing, and even the youngest children take pride in helping others. We need only provide opportunities for them to do the important work that they *already* want to do.

It was becoming clear that I'd been mistaken about my role as director of children's ministries. Caroline, especially, taught me that instead of *delivering* a program to children, maybe I was meant to *empower* them to seek out those in need of their ministry, and to help them be the ministers that I know they are. Not the ministry *to* children, or not only that, but the ministry *of* children.

In chapter 6, I wrote about the importance of recognizing children as full members of the church, particularly as it related to keeping their spaces sacred and honoring their feelings and experiences. This should also include recognizing their capacity to minister to the sick, lonely, grieving, and marginalized in our congregation. A large part of our program is devoted to fostering empathy in children. We practice paying attention to how others are feeling, particularly those who don't often get our attention. We draw children's attention to their suffering, in particular, and we immediately offer opportunities to tend to it. The regularity is important to making it part of children's everyday lives and to making the invisible visible to children. These opportunities to serve others also make children feel like they matter, that their work is meaningful, and that they *do* have the capacity to relieve the suffering of others.

At the end of our first year, Kathy, a member of the pastoral care team and avid gardener, was invited to one of our classes after expressing interest in planting with the children. With Kathy's assistance and humor, children busily decorated flowerpots, filled them with soil, nestled flowers into them, and attached a handmade card to each pot. Kathy explained that she and other members of the pastoral care team would be delivering these flowers to people who were no longer able to come to church. She also told the children about the people who would be receiving the plants and how much it would mean to them to receive a gift from the children of our church.

• •

What does the pastoral care ministry mean for our homebound parishioners? For many it means the world. Most had been very active in the Saint Barnabas community when they were able to attend church on a regular basis. These individuals founded many of our existing ministries and continued some of our legacy community events. For some of them, being shut off from their church family would be akin to a divorce! When we visit, we can offer communion, our prayers, or just a friendly visit, but we are given more in return. This is truly a ministry of our Lord, as it says in the Bible, "For where two or three are gathered in my name, I am there among them" (Matthew 18:20).

Even though members appreciate our pastoral visits, when we include cards, gifts, and messages from our Sunday school children, they are just over the moon with happiness, joy, and even tears—our visit means so much more. Seeing children's church activities relating to their everyday lives justifies our time and hard work to keep the church running for further generations. Indeed it is true, and especially at Saint Barnabas, "It takes a village to raise a child." —Kathy W.

• •

Children were already accustomed to doing projects and activities that benefited those in need, but hearing it from Kathy was still important. The more children hear it, the more they believe it, and the more they know that others believe it too. Even though children love to take projects home, no one asked for a potted plant on this particular day. Instead the children dutifully lined up their freshly painted pots outside the classroom, knowing they would reach a more important place later in the week.

As promised, Kathy reached out to other members of the pastoral care team, letting them know how she and the children spent the morning, and that the offerings would be waiting outside the class-room ready for delivery. The pots disappeared one by one throughout the week as our pastoral care ministers carried off the offerings from our children ministers to our members in need. And a couple of weeks later, of course, the children received notes of gratitude from recipients of some of the potted plants.

In the year that followed, children continued to send cards, along with kindness rocks, hand-painted coffee mugs, and handmade neck warmers for aching muscles. There is no doubt that the children have touched the lives of many others, and no doubt that children feel like they're having an impact on a group of people that they might never get a chance to meet but yet are part of the same community.

Failing to recognize this profound capacity in our children means ignoring one of the church's greatest gifts and some of our most capable and dedicated ministers. This is the best that church has to offer, and there are infinite ways in which it can be done. A mother of a first grader told me she was grateful for a program that is giving her child more opportunities to serve others. Like other parents, she's busy, and doesn't make as much time as she'd like for activities that tend to the suffering of others. She said bringing her child to Sunday school is like "serving more fruits and vegetables, the stuff kids really need. And hopefully making it easier to turn down that Twinkie."

Seek Out the Good Work Already Being Done

Like the work of our pastoral care team, there is great work already being done in your church by committed groups and individuals that complement any children's program. Finding ways to tap into this existing energy and expertise is an easy way to make your children's ministry meaningful to the whole church.

Saint Barnabas is in a small town on Cape Cod, where our population fluctuates between ten thousand and thirty thousand, depending on who you talk to, and whether it's winter or summer. A year ago, a parishioner, Ellie, began to call attention to the problem of homelessness in our town. Whether or not we *had* a homeless population was highly disputed among town officials, but encampments in nearby woods proved that there were indeed a small but real group of people without housing, sleeping outside in the winter and at risk of exposure. Ellie called together others with experience or passion ministering to the homeless, and she worked tirelessly to get a winter housing program for the dozen or so people who would otherwise not be housed through the winter months. Through a lot of hard work and collaboration, the group was able to secure housing for those who needed it, as well as a massive coordinating effort to provide delivered meals to each of the housing locations on a daily basis.

When I learned of this, I met with Ellie to see how our youth group could be helpful to the housing and meal program in a *real* way. Saint Barnabas was responsible for making and delivering meals each Sunday through the winter months, so I signed up our youth group to cook, bake, package, and deliver meals to this group during our winter gatherings. The first time we did this, Matt and I removed the car seats from the minivan and loaded it back up with five middle-school students, who helped us deliver the meals. At each location, kids took turns hopping out of the van to deliver their freshly prepared meals to our neighbors who needed it most. They shook hands, introduced themselves, described the food that was inside, and then hopped back into the van to share their experience with the group. The kids loved it and couldn't wait to do more.

When the Christmas season rolled around, I bumped into Ellie at the church office. She was racing around trying to plan for the next organizational meeting and casually mentioned that someone suggested *she* organize Christmas presents for the residents. Ellie admitted that she simply did not have the time to coordinate such efforts. I offered multiple suggestions, trying to find easy ways to spread the workload so this group could have a Christmas they deserved. Ellie, however, was not persuaded that it would be easy.

I mulled it over and proceeded with caution as we entered mid-December and another chaotic Christmas season. I envisioned breaking the news to Matt that I wanted to organize a Christmas present drive, involve the youth group, and still hold it together at home with decorations, the Santa business, two of our children's birthdays, and both of our jobs that have us working until late Christmas Eve.

I was reminded of Martin Luther King Jr.'s interpretation of the Good Samaritan and how those who ignored the wounded man did so because they thought first about themselves, asking, "What will happen to me if I help this man?" It was the Good Samaritan, King says, who asked himself instead, "What will happen to this man if I *don't* help him?"

So we did it. We cut down a leafless branch from a tree behind the church, spray-painted it glittery white, and strung hearts from the tree with items that our homeless neighbors had requested. I added other items, too, because these folks deserved a Christmas like we were accustomed to having: the one where you get what you *want*, not just what you need. One woman asked for "good smelling soaps," unlike the ones typically donated to homeless shelters. Some asked for things that gave clear indication of what they'd hoped for themselves in the New Year: one woman's request for Jolly Ranchers to quit smoking, and a young man's desire for a toaster oven and utensils anticipating self-sufficiency. An older gentleman requested gifts for his *grandchildren* instead, as if the real gift he wanted was to be able to give to his family.

Our parishioners stripped the tree bare; everyone would be receiving the good smelling soaps, fancy chocolates, and extra gift cards. I couldn't keep up with the line of people waiting to rain blessings upon our neighbors housed through Ellie's efforts.

The following week, items trickled into our office. Overflowing bins lined the hallways, full of generosity and good will. What surprised me most, though, was the number of people who brought in items. Clearly, the Giving Tree hadn't been stripped by a couple of would-be Santa Clauses. On the contrary, it was small efforts by so many people, which resulted in a big impact on the lives of our neighbors who needed us this Christmas season. When items were dropped off, the donor often stopped in to see me, to make sure they got the right item or to ask if I thought the gift would be well received. I heard stories of where they shopped for the item, how many people in their family went with them, and why they picked it out. One gentleman said, "I bought this fellah a pair of nice, wool socks, just like the ones my kids got me last year." One woman, Merrily, drove all over Cape Cod looking for a black, extra-large winter coat to fill a woman's request for a new coat. When she couldn't find one, she ordered it online and worried it wouldn't get here in time to be delivered with the rest of the presents.

In the days before Christmas, children and youth from kindergarten to high school stopped in after school to sort, wrap, tag, and decorate gifts for men and women. Families enthusiastically volunteered to load their cars with bins full of presents and deliver them to our homeless neighbors' temporary homes. Some of the families were told by the residents that these were the only gifts they would be receiving this Christmas, leaving an impression on these youth that would linger through the entire holiday season. There was no doubt that the love that went into the Saint Barnabas Giving Tree was enormous, and that it was already here. It just needed that little nudge.

The good news is that it's waiting to spread in your church, too; you have your *own* version of the Giving Tree. What made it a resounding success was connecting the energy and enthusiasm of our children to a successful ministry in our church. Children were incorporated in a real and tangible way that was meaningful to them, and parishioners were eager to assist the children in helping serve the needs of our homeless neighbors. In fact, it wasn't clear if the involved church members were more motivated to help our children or our homeless ministry. And, in truth, it doesn't matter. What matters is that it was happening, and that many, many people were responsible for spreading love in every which direction during that Christmas season. From Ellie to Merrily and the *literally hundred* adults and children in between, this activity and the wonderful people who participated are *real* church, the kind worth wrestling your children into dress clothes on Sunday mornings.

Child-Initiated Service Projects

Our Giving Tree was such a success that I immediately sought other ways to involve the whole church in the children's upcoming Love Neighbor service projects. It had become clear that something special happens when you invite people to care about something meaningful and give them opportunities to make a positive difference. As we were heading into the unit and teachers had gotten to know their classes better, one of the teachers, Bette, made a point to let me know that her class was particularly interested in animals. She said that despite their differences, the children in this class had connected over a shared affinity for animals. Could they, she asked, do a service project related to animals? Of course they could.

Bette's class spent a couple of weeks talking about abused animals, learning about organizations that care for these animals, and discussing why advocacy is important. Together children made cat and dog toys, folding and cutting, braiding and knotting, using this time to generate something for animals that have suffered, and also connect to one another through a project that felt important to everyone. The children loved this project, and it took no convincing from Bette that loving our neighbor included furry pets; the children already knew that.

Watching Bette and her class work on a project that was important to them confirmed that my role was to learn about what was important to the children, and then find ways for them to serve others. Or better yet, empower teachers to listen to children so together they can find the most meaningful ways to help others.

Jackie's class had a much different dynamic, full of older siblings, making the general tone of the class surprisingly and touchingly nurturing. Their age and personalities made a project helping homeless children in our own community a perfect match for this group. Together this class spent several weeks congregating in small groups on the floor, huddled around large, square pieces of fleece, knotting fuzzy fabric together to make blankets for children living in our local shelter. This project naturally drew out conversations about what it would be like to live in a shelter, or to sleep in your car. We pondered what it means to be loved by God and still have a difficult life, how thankful we were for basic needs like food and shelter, and how we are asked to show God's love to those in need. The children in this class, particularly with this project, understood the importance of what we were doing and that they were showing God's love by tending to the suffering of other children, just like them. One mother pulled me aside after dropping off her six-year-old and said, "You know, I didn't think we were going to come today, but my son told me, 'Mom, it's important,' and so we're here."

I think kids know when adults are genuine and when they're being patronizing—especially when it comes to love. We tell the children the work they're doing is important, and they are easily and quickly convinced. They intuitively know that what they're doing in our Sunday school program tends to real suffering, both inside our community and out. Because it truly does.

A church community is unique, and I often share this with the children. I tell them that our community is committed to serving others, and so what we do for those in need should be shared with other adults in the church so they can participate, too. I talk about increasing the impact of our efforts, how doing so unites and bonds us, and spreads God's love further, wider, and deeper. Turning these projects toward the rest of the congregation is how other adults learn about what the children are doing and gives the whole community the opportunity to serve others alongside the youngest ministers of our parish.

Every chance I get I talk about what we're doing in Sunday school with other members. I want everyone in our church to feel like they're part of our children's ministry in some way, shape, or form. Even if someone can only offer full moral support, I want it. When recruiting volunteers I learned that twenty-seven people wanted to offer support in twenty-seven different ways. I assumed that was true for the rest of the congregation; every hundred people in our church would want to be involved in a hundred different ways, I just needed to figure out how to help them do so.

When classes were working on their service projects, we planned for how we could incorporate more people. Bette's class learned that the animal shelter needed other items like blankets, towels, pillowcases, dog bowls, and laundry detergent. Jackie's class learned that the family shelter could use diapers, pull-ups, new sheets, and pillows. In the same spirit of the Giving Tree, we invited the rest of the congregation to help us do more, to spread our love further.

During our Love Neighbor children's worship service, we blessed the items that the children made and announced that there would be opportunities for the rest of the congregation to support our projects. Outside the church, children had attached hearts to long dowels and poked them into the lawn, as if hearts were sprouting from the wintery grass. On each heart was an item that would complement the children's handcrafted projects, and everyone was invited to find something that they might want to donate to local children and animals in need. And for those not interested in donating items, they could find a heart that says, "Pray for the homeless" or "Pray for animals" because that was important, too. By the time I exited the church, our garden had been picked over and I only noticed a sea of stems poking out of the ground.

In the weeks that followed, our Sunday school rooms were filled with items from the rest of the congregation. Jackie's class spent a morning packing the items into hand-decorated bags, attaching cards that said, "Someone at Saint Barnabas loves you!" and then sat around in a circle to talk about what this experience meant to all of us while children clung to the hand-packed bags. Children shared that it made them happy, grateful, and important to help children in need. When asked how they would feel receiving such a gift if *they* were living in a homeless shelter, children responded the same way, that it would make them feel happy, grateful, and important. We sat around looking at everything we were able to do, how we were able to invite the rest of the congregation to help, and how we were able to do God's work as a community. How do we feel about that, I asked the group?

One child responded, "I feel so proud right now."

Over the course of a year, children's service projects inspired others to donate hundreds—yes, hundreds—of items that paired with our projects, increasing the depth and breadth of our efforts, strengthening our community, and leaving everyone feeling like they were part of something important, that God's love was alive and thriving in these moments of care and concern for those in need.

Despite calling it "Sunday school," the philosophy of our program is that it's not school at all. It's the portion of church where some of our most gifted ministers gather to pray and learn and share. It's not *a* children's ministry, it's the *children's* ministry: where children's ability to *minister* to others is encouraged and nurtured, and where they learn about their capacity to relieve the suffering of others; guided to this holy place by other ministers, their teachers. It's where Caroline intuitively knows what she is able to give Barbara to show her that she cares about her. It's where Kathy takes her knack for training adult ministers to do pastoral care and combines it with her love for gardening and children, expanding the breadth of her work to help both ministries in a meaningful way. And it's where teachers minister to the children who arrive on Sunday mornings, encouraging them and empowering them to use their gifts to minister to those who need their love most.

CHAPTER 8

. . . .

Our Worship

Saint Barnabas was so good about wanting children. The *desire* was there, without a doubt. They were just less skilled about knowing what to do with them. For the seven years I attended Saint Barnabas before taking this job, children had—as they still do—entered the church to join parents for communion following Sunday school. Until last year, children were brought into the church through the back entrance, out of sight; not even *parents* were expecting the arrival of their own children. Announcements would carry on without pause while children milled about in the back of the church looking for their parents in the last few rows. And parents who eventually noticed their children would spend the announcements shushing and settling children in the pews.

This always bothered me. Somehow the implication of children tiptoeing into the back of the church while the service continued was not lost on me. If you were seated in the back few rows, you likely couldn't hear any of the announcements. And if you *weren't* in the back few rows, it's possible you had no idea how many children were at Saint Barnabas. The first year of our program, I decided to have children enter through the side door, which opened into the front of the sanctuary. This was a purposeful change, both for the children, their parents, and for the other adults awaiting us in the church. Children should enter at a time and in a way that doesn't disrupt the service. I also thought the adults and parents should be part of the energy that children bring with them, lovingly receiving them into the church.

On that first day, children waited outside the church in confusion about the new entrance plan. As if to confirm this hunch of mine, one child asked, "Is this so my mom can find me?" When the side doors to the church opened, the children bounded in with infectious excitement, skipping down the aisles looking for parents. Parents, in turn, waved enthusiastically to their children, signaling them over to their pews. The reunion was a joyful one, as it should be. And nothing else could happen in that moment but receive the children into church and await their reuniting with parents. Even the announcements had to wait.

This small change made a big difference to children, parents, and the rest of the congregation. Without our explicitly saying anything to children, they instinctively knew that they were able to make noise coming into the church, that they were able to reunite with their parents with hugs and kisses, and that they were not a bother, but a joy. Parents were able to welcome their children into church without trying to silence them, taking a moment to see the project they've done, or hear about what they discussed in class. And the rest of the congregation could do very little other than watch the stream of children entering and feel as though they, too, were part of the reunion and celebration.

Every Sunday should be a children's Sunday. That doesn't mean that children need to be showcased at each Sunday service, or that everyone in church has to be in the children's program. Rather, it means that every Sunday children should feel welcomed and included, and know that their presence contributes something positive to the whole church.

The Worship Service

People come to church for a variety of reasons, and on any given Sunday morning I can't presume what got someone out their door and through ours. Even so, it's fair to assume that we all come looking for similar things: to be spiritually nourished and to have a community that gives us strength to go into the world to be the disciples God has called us to be. This should be true for any age, including children.

As I previously mentioned, at Saint Barnabas children spend the first portion of the worship service in their classrooms until joining their parents in the church midway through the service. This is not merely because children have short attention spans, although they do. It's actually by design.

For centuries Christian churches have divided their worship services into two parts, much like I've seen at nearly every church I've ever been to. The first part is meant for reflecting upon God's work in our lives and in the world, and upon what God asks of us and expects us to do. This is done through songs of praise, Scripture reading, homilies or sermons, prayer, and creedal confession. All these ritualized activities work to bind the community together. The first part of the worship service, though, is not merely sophisticated *language* about God; it's rooted in ritual, the backbone of any worship service. It is hearing God's Word and discerning how to respond to it in our lives.

This first part of the regular worship service when children are in Sunday school, at least at Saint Barnabas, is not exactly accommodating to children. Reflection upon God's work and what we are doing is often done with language that's not reasonably comprehensible to young children. The readings and sermon of the first part of the worship service are focused on the adults because children are getting an age-appropriate version in their classrooms. Adults get something *they* understand while children get something better tailored to their age.

The overarching goal of Sunday school is to find a way to make the first part of the traditional liturgy accessible to children. Children can do what adults do, like talk about faith and reflect upon readings and lessons, sing songs, and pray. We just need to ensure it is age appropriate and yet still important. We're not doing something different—we're just having church in a way that pays attention to the developmental capacity and limitations of children. Just like most adults want a sermon rather than a storybook, our children have wants and needs we can meet while still achieving the same ends. Providing an age-appropriate portion of the service for children is important, but equally important is maintaining the routine and ritual that prepares them for growing into the full service. Sunday school, just like church, is about building this routine and ritual into our lives.

When children are in their classrooms during the first part of the church service, we endeavor to replicate a parallel experience. Their time together is not solely the business of a Bible story, but dedicated to reflecting upon God's work in our lives and in the world through Scripture and prayer and conversation, and talking more deeply about what God asks of us and expects us to do. Much like what is happening in church, this is done through age-*appropriate* routine and ritual. We commit to keeping the content and language in classrooms suitable for children, too.

In the Episcopal Church, as in many other denominations, lectionary readings are assigned for the church on a three-year cycle. These stories, however, were selected for an adult audience and—quite frankly—not for children. In our children's ministry, we feel free to choose our own lessons to make our way through the Bible in ways that are best for our children. Instead of learning a new story each week, we focus on one per unit and sit with it over the course of several weeks. Each class learns the same lesson, finding new ways to relate to the story—and relate the story to our purpose for gathering.

This time of sharing and reflecting is meant to reflect the building of community that is happening in the church, in ways that validate and give meaning to children's own experiences. Time is spent praying together—for ourselves and for others—in ways that make this an important pastoral moment for teachers and for children. Each classroom has a chalkboard that reads "Our Prayer List," and children are invited to add names before gathering in circle, making this time together even more meaningful. If given the opportunity, children will often share what is happening in their lives, turning these routine moments into an increasingly important ritual as they grow.

The second part of the worship service is the breaking of bread and giving of thanks—or the Eucharist. This is meant for the *whole* church community, including children, which is why it's called *communion*. It makes sense for children to join adults for this portion of the service because we believe it *is* developmentally appropriate. At our special children's services, the communion is developmentally targeted toward children. On any other Sunday morning, though it's not specifically geared toward children per se, they can participate as every other member of the Church; they're not sitting in the pews coloring while the adults participate in communion. Instead, they come to the altar, raise their hands, and participate wholly in this ritual designed for the entire community.

At Saint Barnabas, despite communion feeling like the ancient tradition that it is, we've found that children love it. It's *clear* that they love it, that they care about it, and that they want to do it right. Even a child as young as a year old can proudly walk down the aisle and up to the altar, hands raised and ready to receive the Body of Christ alongside parishioners twenty, fifty, and even ninety years older. Priests and lay people are accustomed to waiting patiently for children to approach the altar rail, passing the chalice to little hands to dip their bread into the wine. Children don't feel rushed or excluded during this ritual. In fact, they feel included in this holiest of intergenerational rituals at Saint Barnabas, a ritual embraced by the whole church.

In my experience, our communion is the most sacred thing that happens at Saint Barnabas. It is full of subtle and overt acts of love and kindness: people stopping on the way back to their pew to hug a friend who lost someone they love, younger parishioners helping an elder parishioner down the aisle, clergy coming down to offer communion to someone who can't make the walk up to the altar, children holding hands on their way up to the altar. These are not merely things that happen before, during, or alongside this holy moment; these *are* the holy moment.

Other traditions might not have communion every week, and not every church structures their worship service this way. What's important is thinking through these same issues at your church so that children's presence correlates to what is developmentally appropriate. This is not a deeply buried topic in church communities; clearly it's important for churches to be welcoming to families however they do it best. Some churches can go to great lengths to make their worship services child friendly or child appropriate. And some, I think, miss the mark. A church down the road has a separate soundproof room in the sanctuary for children and parents, a glass wall separating them from the rest of the congregation. Parents have reported feeling excluded from the service even though it might have stemmed from a genuine interest in accommodating young families.

Perhaps on the other end of the spectrum are the churches that create play spaces in their sanctuaries, sometimes in the front of the church between the pews and the altar. While this is a nice gesture and maybe even a decent idea for some churches, this isn't *always* the best—or only—way to be child friendly. Being child friendly or child appropriate doesn't necessarily mean it must be designed *for* children; your church *can* welcome children in a real way without creating separate play spaces in the sanctuary.

The truth is that the *people* in your church have as much to do with making a space welcoming to children as the physical space itself. Having a church full of people who welcome squawks and giggles might be the best way to make children and their parents feel like they belong in your church. Without those people, it will be a challenge to be truly welcoming at all. And if that's the case in your church, you might want to reconsider if your congregation really *does* want children, because they will come with squawks, giggles, and screams of injustice when they don't get their way.

I vividly remember the day I felt most welcomed at Saint Barnabas. It had nothing to do with bathrooms, play areas, or the rocking chair. Millie was a toddler and Sam was an infant, and I'd spent most of the service wrestling them away from hymnals and regretting even coming in the first place. It felt like too much work for almost no reward. As the service ended and the organ cued up one of my favorite hymns, I longed for a time in my life when I could just hold a hymnal and sing along. Those days were gone, I guessed. At that exact moment, someone tapped me on the shoulder, handed me a hymnal opened to the page of this favorite hymn of mine and whispered, "No one should miss this hymn."

When I arrive to church on any given Sunday morning, I'm not looking to play with my children in the church sanctuary; I want to hold them in the pews. And what I need more than anything is to be received by the people around me as I was before I came with children, with open arms and open hymnals.

Child-Focused Special Services

Besides welcoming and including children in part of every Sunday morning service, you might also want to consider having periodic services that are child-focused. When I accepted this position, the very first thing Patti said to me was, "Let's plan children's services!"

The very next thing to come out of *my* mouth was, "No, I will not." For years we'd had children's services that left many families feeling confused about what it was meant to be. A parent once asked for clarification before taking the week off: "These family services are just regular services with children in the pews, right?"

Mostly, yes.

I walked back my terse response to Patti with a more professional, "Okay, fiiiiine. But only if we can really, I mean *really* do a children's service. You know, a service that *children* would actually enjoy."

And with that, the deal was struck: I would plan the service.

Full disclosure: besides our previous "family services," I'd never *seen* an actual children's service. I know most churches try to do something like this, often having child-friendly services separate from the regular service, with children and parents at one service, and other adults at the "real" service. Saint Barnabas used to do this I'm told, and why it faded away, I'm not sure, but there didn't seem to be much enthusiasm for siphoning off children and families for a separate service. Regardless of what shape these services take, it's clear that they're important to most churches and almost all try some version of a children or family service.

Perhaps having almost no experience with this was a good thing, in the end. I wasn't interested in having a separate service for children and families, since worshiping alongside people of all ages is one of the greatest things about church. Rarely is there anything in our life that is wholly suitable for and thoroughly enjoyed by both a one-year-old and a ninety-year-old. To start planning a children's service by eliminating what we do best seemed like a move in the wrong direction. So it was settled: everyone would be present. Which then raised the question, "Could our children's service genuinely appeal to children *and* adults?"

Even more than planning a service where everyone was present, I was interested in planning a service where children did the work, in a real and authentic way. In Greek, *liturgy* means the work of the people; all people, not just grownups. If children are to be considered full members of the church, adults should not *do* worship *for* children. Just like our children's program isn't something we give to children, but instead the way we help them *do their work,* these services were no different. This service should be for everyone, but done by this group of ministers: our children.

• •

A couple of years ago, attending the family service, I started to get a headache (I'm not ascribing causation) and stepped into the vestibule for some fresh air. While standing there, I heard one of the ushers murmur, "This service is always a zoo." When asked to be a lay eucharistic minister for our last children's service, I said, only half-joking, "That's the only way I'll come to another family service."

I went to serve that day with some trepidation, with the sort of attitude you might have upon entering the yoga studio and discovering that there's a substitute sitting where your favorite teacher should be. Would I get to have my regular, depended upon, looked for, anticipated pleasures?

Here is what I loved about that service:

The playfulness of it all, the joyous surprise of seeing Matt navigating the altar step (and pulpit!) on his knees as he played Zacchaeus in our gospel lesson. Patti entering into the playacting of the gospel . . . at one point Matt gave her a stage direction, and she said, "Oh, should I be Jesus walking up to you? Okay!" It was so perfect and spontaneous, just like kids playing make-believe.

The attention to each moment: Patti took the opportunity to explain what the gospel is, and to hold up the book; these simple, tactile reminders help sometimes even adults. *Oh, yeah. Right. The gospel is Jesus's words, his stories. Right.*

I was surprised at how moved I was watching the faces of the young girls as they stepped up to the altar. I saw their lives unfolding before them, tethered to this moment, grounded in this teaching and this experience of God's grace. I saw the blessing of being invited into this ritual; this reminder that God is always with them, no matter what life may bring to their doors.

And I was moved by the simple elegance of the small boys intincting their wafers (with more ease and focus than many adults, burdened as we often are by self-consciousness and self-doubt). Some seemed new to walking, yet their tiny hands held the wafer with assurance and grace.

This service gave me more than I could have expected. The habitual gave way to improvisation, uncertainty allowed in the new, the fresh, the lively.

As I process out, carrying the cross, the strains of a long forgotten hymn come to my ears and suddenly I'm back in my own child body, learning what it is to be part of this communion, to partake in these rituals, to be loved as one of God's own.

A few moments later, delivering my offering to the basement, I discover that although the celebration had ended, one child is still serving, helping to count the contents of the collection plate. I loved witnessing that inclusion and shepherding of the young even in that practical activity.

This experience opened my heart and reconnected me to the childhood roots of my faith. —Heidi S.

• •

With all hands on deck, from clergy to hospitality to music, we managed to do it. We designed and executed a child-centered worship service that still felt like church for the adults. Children read, sang, ushered, acolyted, greeted, dismissed, read the Scripture; they did all of it and loved it. And as it turned out, the adults loved it, too. In some cases, these services impacted the adults in meaningful and profound ways, so much that everyone started to *look forward* to children's services.

At Saint Barnabas we plan five children's services a year: Christmas, Easter, plus three times throughout the school year, typically one for each unit (e.g., Love Self, Love Neighbor, Love God). For us, this is the ideal number. Any fewer, and they wouldn't feel like a regular part of our children's ministry; any more and they might intrude upon the regular service a hair too often. It was important to me that the congregation be excited and ready when the next children's service rolled around. The perfect number might be different for your church, but I would encourage you to locate this sweet spot because it does make a difference. And if your church is *not* accustomed to doing children's services, you might want to consider trying it. Having a special service that allows children to participate in the sanctuary and to show the congregants what they are doing is invaluable and essential for making your children's ministry part of the whole church.

These services take careful and thoughtful planning and preparation, not unlike the planning of a regular Sunday service, so that should be expected of a children's service too. But it's totally worth it.

Keep It Short

This doesn't simply mean eliminating parts of the service. It means thoughtfully poring over each part so children's attention is sustained throughout. Our normal worship service typically runs one hour and fifteen minutes, and that's just too long for most children. We aim to dismiss our children's services after one hour, not a moment more. If communion is not a regular part of your service, you should aim for forty-five minutes. That means choosing songs that are short, but also easy to sing. It means choosing readings that are short, but also easy to read—and easy to hear. Every minute and every moment counts. Consider it another precious hour and treat it with the same care and love as the Sunday school hour.

Involve Children

Children spend a lot of time watching adults run the services, from preaching to celebrating to reading to ushering. When given the chance, children will happily accept a role typically reserved for adults. Children can and should do all the readings, usher, greet, pass collection plates, and carry crosses. They can act out gospels, dismiss pews, and pass chalices. Our kids have become so accustomed to ushering that it's not unusual to see a gaggle of children dismissing rows, all gathered around for that holy moment where you get to signal to someone else that it's their time to approach the altar.

This is a great way to involve seasoned ushers, like Frank and Lois, and lectors or acolytes who are interested in working with the children in a different capacity. Some of the best interactions between children and adults have been during—or preparing for—these services. A proud lector might not volunteer in the classrooms, but be eager and willing to guide children through this meaningful role, getting to know each other through a shared love of participating in the worship service.

Music

The music for a children's service should always be accessible to the masses. This is not the time for new songs, but rather the time for familiar songs that evoke fond memories in older parishioners, or songs and hymns that should be "in every child's DNA," as Deb, our music director, likes to say. Choosing simple songs or classic songs will keep the service upbeat and might even have the children humming to themselves all week.

Adults love watching children sing, especially in front of the church, and it can bring them such joy. Our children learn one song to sing as a group at each of our children's services because it's always so well received by our congregation and such a wonderful way to unite the community. When we practice in the weeks preceding the children's service, I tell children that this is part of our service to others, in a way. I add that older people love watching children sing, and if our singing will spread love, then we should do it as best as we can. Even our shiest children are easily persuaded by this, and muster the courage to sing along.

At one of our children's services, we invited the rest of the congregation to join in singing a familiar song after the children sang it a couple of times. Much like our mindfulness bell, this was not necessarily meant to continue. But each time we sing a song invariably one child will request that we "get the adults to sing too." And so now we do it every time.

Liturgy

When it comes to children's services, I don't promote eliminating parts of the liturgy. While it might seem necessary to make it a shorter service, I worry that sends the message to everyone that the regular service isn't useful to children, and I simply don't believe that. We're not doing anything that's so overly complicated that children can't understand: we gather, we pray for others, we listen to Bible passages, we sing, we break bread together, and we sing some more. Children can grasp this ritual, and should feel like they're part of it. We need only do it in language that resonates with them.

I think the goal of any children's service should be to bridge the regular service with their developmental stage by making things easier to understand without eliminating them. We are, after all, trying to incorporate ritual into children's lives because we think it serves an important purpose. There are wonderful resources for creative liturgy that are easily accessible and you should work with your pastor or priest to find something that still resonates with the adults in the pews, but is simple enough that the children can understand. We have one or two that we use for all of the services throughout the year; since it works, we keep using it.

• •

At the last children's service of the year, a group of students stood up with posters with a letter on each, spelling out "God is Love." On the back of each poster was written one thing the child had said was an example of God's love. My daughter, Hannah, was holding the letter E, and went last. When it came to her turn, she flipped over her poster and said, "God is there when I smell and touch my mommy's hair." Hannah has been drawn to my hair since she was a baby. I remember her breastfeeding while reaching up with her tiny hand to feel the ends of my hair. She is now seven, and she still touches it when I give her a hug, when she sits on my lap, or when I tuck her in at night. For her to make a connection between this loving gesture and her perception of what God is attests to her learning that God is about a connection rooted in love. —Jennifer P.

• •

Children's Sermons

I've seen plenty of these to know that they are rarely for children. The priest calls up the children to sit at his or her feet while they ask questions with obvious answers, hoping that children will say something funny or cute that gets a good laugh from the congregation. The message is usually intended for adults with children serving as props. While that's quick and easy—and not necessarily wrong—I think children sense that it's not meant for them, that they're not in on the joke. Communicating a message to adults *is* important, but in a way that the children feel like they're really part of it, too. Consider having *children* deliver the lesson or gospel to adults in a way that is fun and interactive. This can be done with advance planning or with spontaneity, depending on your congregation, your children, and your own comfort level.

With some planning, children can prepare for the lesson or gospel ahead of time in any number of ways. The key to making it go smoothly is good narration, which will lead to a good flow. If you have that, then children can do skits, shout out or share examples that correlate with the lesson, or do other unexpected things that keep them engaged and the rest of the congregation captivated.

During one service, the children playfully interrupted Matt while he pretended to be giving a boring sermon. As you might expect, the children loved (like so, so much) pretending to fall asleep to the sermon, some loudly snoring and hunching over in the pews. They finished the lesson by testing his knowledge about loving our neighbor with a game show–style quiz. And of course, the children won.

At our children's services, there's no mistaking that children are primarily responsible for delivering the sermon. They know it, and everyone else knows it too. And this isn't a ruse; children can *actually* give a powerful and effective sermon with a bit of planning and good direction.

If you prefer spontaneity, children can easily act out parts of the gospel lesson with the right narrator to guide them. On Christmas and Easter, we do a pick-up pageant where the children volunteer on the spot and are seamlessly (usually) incorporated into the lesson. Spontaneity allows for playful confusion and mistakes that leave people feeling like they're part of the planning and part of the fun—and no one will expect a perfect show. However you decide to do it, the important thing is that children be involved in *presenting* the message, not having the message presented to them.

Make It Meaningful

Just like our precious hour in the classrooms, we still commit to protecting every minute we spend with children. As such, everything in these worship services has to serve the purpose of being child-centered: every reading, every song, every word, and every transition. Furthermore, the service needs to mirror what the children have been learning in their classes, as this worship service is our opportunity to share with the rest of the congregation what we've been doing.

As mentioned in chapter 7, during one of the children's services we brought in all the items we'd made for children in homeless shelters, and for animals in pet shelters. Together as a congregation, and following the children's lead, we blessed these items before sending them out into our community. We also use these services as a chance for children to describe what they've learned, which has included discovering what they think is most lovable about themselves, and naming those moments when they feel God's presence. This is how the adults learn about what the children are doing, and how children learn that adults *care* about what they're learning.

Fold It In

In each service, I make sure there's an opportunity for the rest of the congregation to participate in whatever the children are doing, whether they, too, are naming out loud what makes them lovable or where they find God, or singing together a song in rounds. The children don't perform (and I tell them this all the time) but are sharing what they've learned and inviting the rest of the church to join in.

As a gift to your church, you might want to consider having special services throughout the year that allow children to participate in the sanctuary and to show what they are doing during Sunday school. It works; not only does the congregation feel connected to what the children are sharing, but the children quickly understand their role is to initiate a song or a conversation that will incorporate the whole church, that their work on these mornings is to do the service themselves for the adults—and for real.

If this sounds familiar, it's because you've heard it in every previous chapter. This is the whole shtick. This is what I think should be done with every single part of a children's ministry: fold it into the rest of the church. Make the children's ministry part of every other ministry, and invite other ministries to participate in yours. Your children's ministry is not *just* for children, or parents, or teachers—it's for the whole church.

Epilogue

In September of 2017, we began our second year of Love First with neat and tidy classrooms, rested teachers, and a great deal of positive energy from the previous year. We opened the doors to our building and welcomed new and returning families with a simple sign that read, "We LOVE that you're here." This time, though, it felt different. It felt like we didn't have to convince anyone; they already knew it was true.

Returning children had clear expectations of what would be happening in Sunday school, and new children were easily convinced. We welcomed everyone, not knowing exactly what the year would bring, but that people were returning because they were ready to love some more. And so were we.

We were moving forward, taking with us everything we'd learned from people like Bette, who is still involved with our program as an environmental guru; Caroline, who continues to stop at Barbara's pew to greet her when she enters the church; Flannery, who returned for another year knowing that she was the perfect fit; and Frank, who is already signed up for every children's service this year.

A few weeks before we opened the doors, our senior warden, Sue, asked me what I had planned to do for the upcoming Sunday school year. She asked in a way that hinted she wanted to know what the *second* year of our new curriculum would look like. For clarification, I asked, "You mean, is there a Year #2 in this curriculum *after* Love Self, Love Neighbor, Love God?

"Yes," she said.

I told her, "Sue, show me a child that doesn't need more loving self, loving neighbor, or loving God and I'll write you a whole new curriculum for next year."

Love First doesn't have an ending. In fact, it seems to be spreading. Parents are reporting that they're able to approach their children in different ways, leading with love instead of impatience and frustration, and finding that problems look different and less challenging through this compassionate lens. More adults are talking about and expressing love, so much that newcomers' first impressions of Saint Barnabas have less to do with our beautiful buildings and more to do with how loving our community feels, getting us a little closer to being the community that Jesus asked us to be.

During a getting-to-know-you exercise in the first few weeks of the year, a six-year-old boy came up to me and said, "I bet I know your favorite holiday." I wasn't sure what he meant and so I asked him, "What do you mean?" He responded, "It's probably Valentine's Day because it's all about love." This was one of the best things I heard all year and proof that keeping it simple, keeping it meaningful, and keeping it about love meant that this little guy totally understood what happens when we gather at church.

APPENDIX A

• •

Heartbeats

At Saint Barnabas, we used the Love First model to develop our own curriculum that embraced the gifts of our church. Offering *our* curriculum to other churches gives the impression that our gifts are your gifts, and that there is not self-reflection and deep exploration that necessarily *must* come first. Therefore, what we have to offer below are not lesson plans, but what we like to call "heartbeats." When discovering the path to our own curriculum, we began with a simple—though essential—heartbeat. These are distillations of scriptural passages that you can build several lessons or weeks around, depending upon the talent and interests of the teachers and students, the ages and abilities of the students, and the size and age-span of each class.

Each heartbeat is an essential component to the Love First program, but not the *only* component. For a heartbeat to work, you need the rest of the body: eyes, ears, brain, legs, and so on. Using your community's talents, interests, and gifts, these heartbeats can come alive in your church—and in the people who participate. It is up to each church, each children's ministry team, to make these heartbeats something that breathes life into your faith community.

In each heartbeat we offer the teacher a passage from Scripture, and then describe the heart of the scriptural teaching, which then can serve as the heartbeat for each class's lessons, activities, prayers, and reflections for each day the lesson is used. Also, this ensures that these passages take a deep dive, which means our teachers might spend four to six weeks on one heartbeat, doing different activities, incorporating gifts of the congregation, and using contemporary literature to complement the Scripture.

Because Love First depends upon our teachers to bring their gifts and talents to each gathering, every class looks different as far as how the heartbeat is presented and practiced. Some teachers prefer to read the parable; others will use puppets, peg dolls, felt boards, or skits; older children can locate the Scripture in the Bible and read together. The first few weeks, we dig into the Scripture so children have a clear sense of what the text is saying. We do this through repetition, by presenting the story in a new way—or even in the same way—and by asking further questions about the characters, what they might be thinking and how they might have arrived at the decisions that they made, looking at each character—even those who are cruel or hurtful—through the lens of love.

In the weeks that follow, we find contemporary literature to explore the same themes, but make it real to children in their contemporary lives. Contemporary books that reinforce the themes of Scripture are being published at a rate that makes it easy for teachers to find something just right for the children in front of us at that moment in time. Our goal in selecting books is not always to portray exemplary characters of Jesus's discipleship, but rather to find books that spark conversation about how some characters or stories do *not* live up to what Jesus is asking of us.

For each heartbeat, teachers select projects that make the heart of the Scripture come alive in the classrooms and in children's lives, incorporating the gifts of other congregants into projects that don't only complement the heartbeat, but build relationships too.

If a simple craft activity is the most suitable way for you to reinforce the heartbeat, there is no end to the resources found on Pinterest or other websites that fit your interests, budget, and needs. Find ways to tap into the creativity of others who are willing to share their ideas.

As a reminder, discipleship is a practice and a habit. Therefore we don't just encourage repetition, we embrace it wholeheartedly and find it another essential element of children's formation. Recurring activities are found throughout our children's ministry as long as they continue to give children opportunities to bring meaning to their lives, and deepen their relationship with God and one another.

Most importantly, keep in mind that what works for us might not work for you, and vice versa. You know your community best, and you will learn—as you go—what works well, what doesn't, and what needs to be fine-tuned. As teachers, formation ministers, or rectors, we are always learning too, which is how a children's ministry will evolve— over time—into something that's not just for children or their teachers, but for the whole church.

Love Self: The Healing of the Paralyzed Man and the Call of Matthew (Matthew 9:2–13)

The Heart of the Scripture

There are several stories of healing throughout the gospels, and in any of them we have the opportunity to speak with children about issues of wellness and sickness, especially if some of your children have loved ones who are ailing or suffering. You can use these lessons to reassure these and all children that God cares for us and seeks our healing, provided that any overly simplistic morals are avoided, since in some cases your children's loved one may not find physical healing; these sadnesses need not be an occasion to question God's love and care. Use some caution in these stories, because you don't want to give your children the impression that physical ability or well-being is the only sign of God's love. It's also important to note that, in Jesus's day, bad fortune was understood to be judgment from God. Many people would have assumed that the paralyzed man was a sinner, just as the tax collector Matthew was seen as a sinner. But Jesus loves them anyway. These details can help you speak with your children about reserving judgment and about reaching out to others who have been cast aside. In fact, part of what's useful about the first half of this story is that Jesus cares about the paralyzed man's heart, not his physical ability.

This story of healing can be useful for you in helping children see the reach of God's love; it extends across all sorts of difference. For older children, it might be suitable to show how this story also extends the ministry of Jesus to all of us as Jesus's disciples. When Jesus heals the paralyzed man here, he tells him that his sins are forgiven. The scribes call this blasphemy, because in their opinion only God can forgive sins. But Jesus insists that this work is his own. This is important because it further reveals the truth of the Incarnation in Matthew: that Jesus is and has the power of God. But it's especially important for us as his followers, because Jesus tells us that *we* have the power to forgive sins too, later on. Our work, the work of forgiving sins and of serving others, is God's work too. God is alive in us when we perform Jesus's ministry. So there are several ways you can affirm the worth and ministry of children in this story, not only by assuring them that they are always infinitely loveable, however they are and whoever they are, but also by encouraging them to feel empowered by that love to share it with others.

Other readings which share this heartbeat
Any books or stories that speak to the innate lovability and worth of every child, especially despite social or physical differences. This could and should include stories that demonstrate graciousness and kindness in reaching out to strangers or outcasts, or about reserving judgment and forgiveness, such as:

God chooses David over his brothers (1 Samuel 16:1–13)

Blind Bartimaeus (Mark 10:46–52)

The wedding feast (Luke 14:7–14)

Zacchaeus (Luke 19:1–10)

Barroux. *Welcome*. Hampshire, UK: Egmont Books Ltd, 2016.

Graham, Bob. *How to Heal a Broken Wing*. Somerville, MA: Candlewick Press, 2008.

Ludwig, Trudy. *The Invisible Boy*. New York: Penguin Random House, 2013.

Palacio, R. J. *Wonder*. New York: Penguin Random House, 2012.

Goeminne, Siska. *No One Else Like You*. Louisville, KY: Westminster John Knox Press, 2016.

Turner, Matthew P. *When God Made You*. Colorado Springs, CO: WaterBrook, 2017.

Making it part of the whole church
This is a great time to invite parishioners into your classrooms who have a special gift or interest that—at first glance—might not seem

relevant to a children's ministry. When adults show children that they love themselves, even the quirky or odd parts, this can help children accept parts of themselves, too, that don't always get the positive attention they need.

Christmas

The Heart of the Scripture

The lesson of the Christmas story may seem obvious, perhaps, but there are several things you can and should do to make this lesson real for your children. The meaning of incarnation is not just that God became human two thousand years ago, but also that Christ remains alive in us and in our ministry today, as well as alive in the people we serve. The promises of our Baptismal Covenant—to share in fellowship, to persist in repentance, to proclaim Christ in our lives, to seek and serve Christ in all persons, to strive for justice—these are directly related to the feast of Incarnation, because we are the Body of Christ. So when we show mercy, say we're sorry, or forgive others' wrongs or help those who are suffering, we are living into the story of Christmas. This can be a truly empowering lesson for children, one that can help them understand themselves as full disciples and the Christmas story as fundamentally about their own lives as Christians.

Other readings which share this heartbeat

Any books or stories that help children think through what it means to "seek and serve Christ in all persons," such as:

Hardie, Jill. *The Sparkle Box: A Gift with the Power to Change Christmas.* Nashville, TN: Ideals Children's Books, 2012.

Spinelli, Ellen. *Somebody Loves You, Mr. Hatch.* New York: Simon and Schuster Books, 1996.

Vivas, Julie. *The Nativity.* Boston: Houghton Mifflin Harcourt, 2006.

Williams, Laura E. *The Can Man.* New York: Lee & Low Books, 2017.

Woodson, Jacqueline. *Each Kindness.* New York: Nancy Paulsen Books, 2012.

Making it for the whole church

Christmas is an ideal time to partner with other ministries that offer or arrange gifts, financial assistance, winter clothing, or housing to those in need.

Love Neighbor: The Good Samaritan (Luke 10:25–37)

The Heart of the Scripture

Although this story is familiar to most Christians, and though its general lesson of help toward strangers is a familiar and appropriate one, there are details to this lesson which can dramatically affect your interpretation of it and offer great possibilities for conversation, reflection, role play, and service among your students.

In the Gospel of Luke, this parable is meant to illuminate Jesus's teaching that the heartbeat of all of Scripture is to love God, and to love your neighbor as yourself. (It's not an accident we've structured our church school year around these three loves!) A lawyer, being lawyerly, is concerned to know the details of this teaching. "Who is my neighbor?" the lawyer asks, evidently hoping to fulfill only his technical ethical obligations and no more. So Jesus tells this story in response.

It's important to think about the category of neighbor. In the ancient world, moral obligations tended to be aligned with social roles: you were differently obligated toward citizens than you were toward slaves, toward Jews than you were toward Gentiles, toward men than you were toward women. Jesus is saying those social stratifications don't matter; we are obligated toward whoever we're close to. That's what neighbor means, literally: the one nearby. And this is dramatically rendered in the story because a Samaritan was considered a religious heretic for Judeans of the day.

It's also important therefore that the priest and Levite of the story cross the road to stay away from the beaten Judean man, but that the Samaritan goes directly to him. The priest and Levite create distance; the Samaritan comes close, he makes the beaten man his neighbor. So Jesus isn't just saying, "Love your neighbor," he's also saying, "Make those who are in need and in trouble your neighbors so you can love them."

Last, we should also think as generously as we can about the priest and Levite. They were religiously forbidden from touching blood—if they did they were not allowed to offer sacrifice at the Temple. So the priest and Levite are actually following religious rules in this case, not just being heartless strangers. This can be a useful way to think about how our own religious practices might keep us from living Jesus's teachings.

Martin Luther King Jr. invites us to soften our hearts further with the priest and Levite, looking at them through the lens of love. In his final speech before his assassination, "I've Been to the Mountaintop," King imagined that the priest and Levite were not merely worried about their religious duties, but may have been genuinely scared to go toward the Judean. The road to Jericho was indeed risky, and helping a man in the road could have been a trap to lure them into danger. Despite the reasons for not helping the Judean, King imagines that the priest and Levite asked, "If I stop to help this man, what will happen to me?" while the Samaritan asked, "If I do not stop to help this man, what will happen to him?"[1]

Other readings which share this heartbeat
Any books or stories which celebrate difference or find beauty in it, or which show characters reaching across social divides, such as:

Abraham and the three strangers (Genesis 18:1–15)

Elijah and the widow at Zaraphath (1 Kings 17:7–16)

The prodigal son (Luke 15:11–32)

Jonah at Nineveh (Jonah 3–4)

Boelts, Maribeth. *Those Shoes.* Somerville, MA: Candlewick Press, 2007.

Dobrin, Arthur. *Love Your Neighbor: Stories of Values and Virtues.* New York: Scholastic, 1999.

Fox, Mem. *Wilfrid Gordon McDonald Partridge.* Brooklyn, NY: Kane/Miller Book Publishers, 1989.

Lamothe, Matt. *This is How We Do It.* San Francisco: Chronicle Books, 2017.

---

1. Martin Luther King Jr., "I've Been to the Mountaintop" (speech, Memphis, TN, April 3, 1968), American Rhetoric, http://www.americanrhetoric.com/speeches/mlkivebeentothemountaintop.htm.

Woodson, Jacqueline. *The Other Side*. New York: G. P. Putnam's
Sons, 2001.

Making it for the whole church
At any given moment, there is someone in your church who needs
to be served. Find ways to let the children minister to these people
in meaningful ways, whether it's sending cards, making gifts, saying
prayers, or inviting them into the classrooms so children can get to
know them and vice versa. Children like to know why they are reaching out to other parishioners, which also provides opportunities to talk
about grief, sickness, addiction, death, oppression, or marginalization
in a way that makes recipients of these gifts not only visible but meaningful to children.

Easter

The Heart of the Scripture
Much like Christmas, the meaning of the Easter story might seem obvious to you or to your faith community, but it might not be obvious to
your children. However, it can be made real for them in engaging ways.
The story of Jesus's death can be an important lesson through which
to speak with your children about death, failure, and grief, as well as
about what these things might mean to them. These discussions about
children's fears and bereavements are not meant to be merely thera-
peutic, however. Theologically they can serve as a useful entry point
into what may be the richest part of this the Easter story: the fear and
uncertainty that Jesus's death *and resurrection* stir in his friends and
followers. In the Gospel of John, Jesus calls Peter to discipleship again,
despite his fear and failure. In the Gospel of Mark, the women come
to care for Jesus's body on Easter morning even though they are sad
and scared. Mary weeps when the tomb is empty in John. The Easter
story thus provides an opportunity to speak with your children about
discipleship as the willingness to follow Jesus—that is, to love God and
our neighbors and ourselves—even when doing so feels scary or hard
or impossible, or even after we've failed to do so in the past.

Language about Jesus's death should be handled carefully. That
Jesus died for our sins is important, but the church has often unnec-

essarily conveyed this as a message of shame and punishment rather than as one of love and new life. The subtleties, complexities, and nuances of atonement theology can and should, we think, be saved for adolescents who are more capable of abstract and critical thought. Because the most important theological promise of Easter, for children and for adults, is that Christ's death and resurrection make him alive in us as his church today, as Christ's risen body here and now. So, much like Christmas, the Easter story is an opportunity to encourage children to live into their baptismal promises, and to tell them that Christ lives in them and in the neighbors they serve, and in the ministries of the Church.

Other readings which share this heartbeat

Any books or stories that discuss fear, grief, or other negative emotions with hopefulness and love, any stories about new life springing from loss, or stories which illustrate what it means to "seek and serve Christ in all persons."

Coles, Robert. *The Story of Ruby Bridges*. New York: Scholastic Paperbacks, 2010.

de la Peña, Matt. *Last Stop on Market Street*. New York: Penguin Random House, 2015.

Patel, Andrea. *On That Day*. Berkeley, CA: Tricycle Press, 2001.

Stead, Philip C. *A Sick Day for Amos McGee*. New York: Macmillan Publishers, 2010.

Williams, Vera B. *A Chair for My Mother*. New York: Greenwillow Books, 2007.

Yamada, Kobi. *What Do You Do With a Problem?* Seattle, WA: Compendium, Inc., 2016.

Making it for the whole church

Consider introducing foot washing with children in the weeks preceding Easter as a way to think more deeply about Jesus and the many ways he took care of others. Invite parishioners into the classroom, either to receive foot washings or to wash feet. Whether a child participates or not, this activity can generate rich conversation about Jesus, about themselves, and about the courage it can take to serve those who need us most.

Love God: Jesus has breakfast with Peter after Easter (John 21:9–17)

The Heart of the Scripture

The temptation after Easter is to believe that the story has ended with its fairy tale ending: Jesus is raised from the dead and they all lived happily ever after. The story is much more complex than this and children can and should bear this complexity and reflect upon what it means for their lives. Resurrection stories are especially suitable for helping children consider the third, and most abstract, pillar of the Love First framework: Love God. It's worth reminding children of what you may have already discussed during Easter: that all Jesus's friends abandoned him when he got into trouble. What you have been remembering all year is reaffirmed here when Jesus returns to his friends and invites them to breakfast: Jesus loves us even when we let him down. Faith means trusting that we are always lovable, and that God loves us. And this becomes the point at which this passage, and your discussions, can pivot toward the love of God. "Love God" *is* somewhat abstract, but the beauty of this passage is that Jesus makes this task very concrete for Peter and for us. Jesus asks Peter three times if Peter loves him, and each time Peter replies yes, Jesus responds: "Feed my sheep." Little children will of course need to be told the sheep here aren't literal; you might even remove the metaphor in your retelling of this story and say something like, "Care for my people," instead; or even (from earlier in John) the famous final commandment "Love one another." Either way, what you are showing children is that we show our love for God in how we love one another. In subsequent lessons on this Scripture, encourage children to name the places in their lives where they see and feel love, and help them identify the presence of God in those places. Overall, the aim is to encourage children to recognize God's love already at work in their lives. This is an excellent capstone lesson because it shows how all three units in the program—Love Self, Love Neighbor, Love God—support one another. God loves us because we are always lovable, and we love God in the love we show to others.

Other readings which share this heartbeat
Any books or stories that discuss the different ways we can think about and encounter God, or books about love, especially ones that describe love as its own reward, rather than as the means to some other end.

The prophetic call to love (Hosea 6 and/or Micah 6)

The Beatitudes (Matthew 5:1–12)

Two disciples on the road to Emmaus (Luke 24:13–35)

Bergen, Lisa T. *God Gave Us Love.* Colorado Springs, CO: WaterBrook Press, 2009.

de la Peña, Matt. *Love.* New York: G. P. Putnam's Sons, 2018.

Grant, Jennifer. *Maybe God Is Like That Too.* Minneapolis, MN: Sparkhouse, 2017.

Lloyd-Jones, Sally. *Baby Wren and the Great Gift.* Grand Rapids, MI: Zonderkidz.

Tutu, Desmond. *God's Dream.* Somerville, MA: Candlewick Press, 2008.

Making it for the whole church
When exploring ways to communicate with God through differing forms of prayer, invite children to pray for parishioners who are on the wider church prayer list. Children can make multiple sets of prayer beads and share them with other adults sitting in the pews, and older children—or the entire class—can write and read the Prayers of the People.

APPENDIX B

• •

Suggested Bible Stories

The Bible is an endlessly complicated compilation of writings, diverse in genre, style, content, interpretation, and history. This means it can be confusing, challenging, and downright mysterious at times, to say the least. Christians regard the Bible as sacred, but often opinions about biblical interpretation and usage devolve into arguments over literal or figurative readings. At Saint Barnabas we like to say that our job as Christians is to take the Bible not just literally or figuratively, but *seriously*. That means reading a story sometimes literally or sometimes figuratively, but mostly being honest about what is confusing, challenging, and mysterious about the sacred text. Nothing should surprise those who place their faith in a God who is at times mysterious, challenging, and even confusing. Faith is a serious thing; it doesn't seek to oversimplify, but recognizes complexity when it sees it and tries to reckon with its mysteries honestly and openly.

What does this mean when we choose to share our sacred texts with our children? We should be alert to the pastoral appropriateness of the stories we decide to tell. It may not be pastorally appropriate to read the story of David and Bathsheba at a wedding or the story of Judith at a prayer service for peace; we should use both our spiritual and pastoral judgment when sharing the Bible's wisdom with children. Just because little children love animals, and little boys love action stories, some biblical stories may not be developmentally appropriate.

In a curriculum built around compassion, there are aspects of those stories—God's choice to destroy all of creation, the rout of the Philistines—may be best left to a later stage of our children's spiritual and emotional development. This is not to imply that any part of the Bible is dispensable or irrelevant, only that we can be more careful and judicious about the developmental, pedagogical, spiritual, and pastoral standards we use when choosing the stories we will tell during our one precious hour.

When you tell these stories, retell them in your own way with felt characters, puppets, wooden dolls, or even in your own words. This will help you place emphasis where it is appropriate for your children, and also help them respond and engage with you in telling the story.

The Hebrew Scriptures

Some of the stories below are familiar, others less so; some of these choices may be expected, others quite surprising. As in all cases, what and how you emphasize aspects of the stories will be what's most important. I've annotated these stories to help you frame your own retellings of them.

Genesis 4:1–16 (Cain and Abel)

This is likely to be a surprising choice after everything I've just said about developmental appropriateness. How could the story of the first murder be an example of developmental or pastoral appropriateness? So I don't suggest this for preschoolers, but as older children may see far worse examples of violence in the media they consume, this story can be important and revealing because God expressly forbids any act of vengeance against Cain after the murder. This can therefore be a helpful story, when used appropriately, for generating conversations about revenge, punishment, and even forgiveness.

Genesis 18:1–15 (Abraham and the Three Strangers)

Our focus in this story is naturally drawn toward the promise of Sarah's miraculous conception and her laughter at that promise. But that miracle is meant to bless Abraham's act of hospitality toward the three strangers that arrive unannounced at his camp, and whom

121

he serves graciously. This can be a good story to help children think about the meaning of hospitality, and what blessings it might bestow upon hosts.

Genesis 45:1–15 (Joseph Forgives his Brothers)
The Joseph story is long and complex, and admittedly loses some of its impact when scenes are excerpted such as this. But if you can summarize the background for your students—that Joseph was cruelly betrayed by his brothers and now finds himself with power over them—then this can be a helpful text in encouraging children to think about forgiveness and reconciliation, especially among family members.

Exodus 3:1–12 (The Call of Moses)
The Moses story and the story of Israel's flight from Egypt is of course in many ways the central and structuring narrative of the entire Hebrew Scripture. Much like the Joseph story, it doesn't gain much by truncation, but there are aspects to this story (the killing of Egypt's firstborn, for example) that children should wrestle with at a later stage of spiritual development. Here, we should encourage children to think about God's choice of Moses, who at the time was a criminal, fugitive, refugee, and didn't believe much in himself. This story can spur discussion about whom God chooses and why, and can lead to lessons about withholding judgment of others or even about self-esteem and self-confidence. It could also, with older children, be used as analogy for discussions of great American leaders who worked to free people from bondage, such as Harriet Tubman.

1 Samuel 16:1–13 (God Chooses David Over his Brothers)
Children's Bibles often include the story of Goliath because it shows God's favor toward the weak or small. But the same lesson can be conveyed without also raising complicated questions of war and ethnic violence by discussing God's favor toward David, even though he was the youngest and smallest of his brothers. Children are used to being overlooked because they are small, and will have a lot to share when hearing this story.

I Samuel 25:1–35 (David and Abigail)

David is a complicated, and sometimes unsavory, biblical figure who often runs afoul of God's wishes. This story is a complicated one too, and will demand some context and perhaps should be reserved for older children. Nabal's rejection of David's request for help after David had protected Nabal's shepherds (along with David's subsequent vengefulness) can help children think about anger and negative emotions. What should be emphasized is Abigail's work as a peacekeeper, and how she was able to keep a rich miser and an enraged king from acting out in violence toward one another.

I Kings 17:7–16 (Elijah and the Widow at Zaraphath)

This story in many ways follows the story of Abraham and the three strangers, and might be used in conjunction with that one. Again, the tendency will be to focus upon the miracle that concludes the story, but children's attention should be drawn to the widow's generosity, in sharing her and her son's last bit of food with a stranger.

Jonah 3–4 (Jonah at Nineveh)

The story of Jonah often is taught to children, mostly because it involves a whale and a fantastical sea voyage. The more important aspect to the story in terms of teaching empathy to children, however, has to do with Jonah's eventual arrival at Nineveh, the city of his enemy, God's promise to love even those Jonah hates, and God's command that Jonah serve God's beloved, even if they are Jonah's enemies.

Hosea 6 and Micah 6 (God wants us to love)

Narrative passages of the Bible will tend to work better than didactic ones, since they generate discussion in more imaginative ways. But upon occasion you might want to look at scriptural texts that speak more directly, especially when discussing what it means to love God. Hosea and Micah, who see love of neighbor as the truest expression of love of God, can be very useful in the classroom.

The New Testament

In some ways the New Testament more directly maps onto the aims of the Love First curriculum, since it is primarily based upon Jesus's teaching and fulfillment of the Hebrew Scriptures in the gospel of love. These stories may be more familiar, but I've included some annotations to clarify interpretive emphasis. You'll recognize a number from the Gospel of Luke. This is not to privilege the portrait of Jesus that Luke paints over the other gospel writers, only to acknowledge that Luke's emphasis on Jesus's teachings and acts of empathy, mercy, and love resonate particularly well with the Love First program.

Matthew 5:1–12 (The Beatitudes)
Stories will generally be more imaginatively useful in your classroom for generating discussion, and there are plenty of stories of Jesus and stories by Jesus to fill your precious hours. But the Beatitudes are such a startling teaching if you think about it. They turn our expectations so completely upside down, and so firmly undergird so much of Christian teaching that they are a useful tool of instruction for Christians of any age.

Mark 10:46–52 (Blind Bartimaeus)
This is another healing story, but again, the emphasis should be on the characters in the situation, rather than on the miracle itself. The crowd orders Bartimaeus to be quiet and orders him not to bother Jesus, but Jesus attends to him and cares for him. Ask students what the people in the crowd might have been thinking, what Bartimaeus's thoughts might have been, or why Jesus decided to listen even though the crowd told him not to. This story could also lead to useful discussions of peer pressure, or of reacting to and resisting the crowds around us.

Mark 12:41–44 (The Widow's Mite)
The story of the widow's meager offering and how it exceeds the rich man's gift could be used to encourage discussions of wealth, worth, and thankfulness.

Luke 14:7–14 (The Wedding Feast)

Matthew also has a version of this parable, but the king reacts much more violently to the absence of his invited guests in that account. Luke's emphasis is upon the poor and disabled who join the feast, and that should be your emphasis too. Ask children to think about what it means to be thankful, who is and isn't included in our celebrations, or even our churches or wider community.

Luke 15:11–32 (The Prodigal Son)

This is the foundational parable of forgiveness in all the gospels, and as such is the perfect story for discussing that topic. Draw attention to the less noticed details: the man runs to his son and embraces him before the son even apologizes; the brother is resentful and impatient at the son's return. Much like the Samaritan story, invite children to imagine themselves into the different roles—the prodigal, his father, the brother—and help them explore their ideas and feelings about forgiveness as they do.

Luke 19:1–10 (Zacchaeus)

This is another story about Jesus paying attention to those whom others resent or refuse to acknowledge. It's much like the story of Matthew's call, but the details here—Zacchaeus's short stature, Jesus's insistence that he stay at Zacchaeus's house, and Zacchaeus's generosity in the end—all make this a great story for role playing or conversation.

Luke 7:1–10 (Healing the Centurion's Servant)

Another story of a healing. Often we emphasize the theme of obedience in this story, and although that may be something children want to discuss, try to draw their attention to the social details here again. This centurion's job was to hurt Jesus and his followers. What does it mean that this centurion didn't? To whom was he really obedient if he wasn't doing his job? To whom are we supposed to be obedient? And how did Jesus treat this man who should have been his enemy?

Luke 24:13–35 (The Road to Emmaus)

This is a useful story after Easter. Saint Barnabas encourages children to think about the Resurrection in terms of love—that Christ lives where love lives. That lesson can help you draw children's attention to the disciples' hospitality here: they are in danger, they're running away, but they're also willing to offer care and safety to a stranger in spite of those things. And when they love first—instead of judging or fearing first—Jesus is there.

John 8:1–11 (The Woman Caught in Adultery)

Because the sin in this case is adultery, we often avoid talking to children about this story. That's a shame, because the nature of the sin is a detail not necessary to the larger lesson of the story. Indeed, even among adults the historical context of sexual roles and practices in ancient Judea is a tangle not easily undone. So when you retell this, feel free to describe the sin however you feel is appropriate (you might say that the woman broke a promise or hurt someone) and focus instead upon Jesus's reluctance to judge, the eagerness of everyone to punish, and the question he poses to the men who wanted to kill the woman.

APPENDIX C

• •

Recommended Book List[1]

The gospel message can be lived and recognized in all sorts of places, including contemporary literature. Below is a list of books that complement the Love First program. This list of books aims to spark meaningful conversations that address loving ourselves, loving others, and loving God, including love, death and loss, poverty, war, friendship, and hope. An additional benefit to using contemporary literature is it often includes attractive illustrations and characters that are more relatable to children and often difficult to find in children's Bibles.

Board Books

Bergren, Lisa T. *God Gave Us Love.* Boulder, CO: Waterbrook, 2011.

When disturbed by pesky otters, little polar bear asks his grandfather why they must love *everyone.* The grandfather's simple answer is easy enough for all ages to understand and a good conversation for even our youngest children: when we love others, we share God's love.

---

1. Special thanks to Stephanie Seales at the Falmouth Racial Justice League and Falmouth Public Library for expert counsel on book lists that foster empathy for children and youth.

Lord, Jill R. *If Jesus Lived Inside My Heart*. Nashville, TN: Candy Cane Press, 2012.

This book is useful for helping younger children understand who Jesus was and what he asked us to do. Through examples of kindness and love, children can talk about what it means to have Jesus living inside our hearts.

Precious Moments: Little Book of Prayers. Nashville, TN: Thomas Nelson Publishers, 2013.

A sturdy prayer book that has prayers for all occasions: morning, bedtime, dinnertime, school, friends, and animals. Written in simple rhyme, these prayers are short and easy to comprehend for even the youngest of children.

Scanlon, Liz G. *All the World*. New York: Little Simon, 2015.

All the World follows a family throughout the day, drawing attention to all things great and small through simple yet profound rhymes. Encourage children to name the small things that they love, and the big things, too. Draw connections to the importance of caring for all the things that we—and others—love.

Picture Books

Amini, Mehrdokht. *Golden Domes and Silver Lanterns*. San Francisco: Chronicle Books, 2012.

This is a basic presentation of Islam and is especially appropriate for children who are not exposed to other Muslim children. It is especially helpful to notice the similarities, not necessarily the differences, among Muslim and Christian children. For example, praying, going to a special building to gather, special desserts for holidays, giving to those in need, and a sacred text.

Barroux. *Welcome*. Hampshire, UK: Egmont Books Ltd, 2016.

Inspired by the Syrian refugee crisis, *Welcome* promotes welcoming and inclusiveness for children. Encourage children to ponder what it would feel like to be the polar bears, especially when the reasons for turning them away don't seem fair or just.

Boelts, Maribeth. *Those Shoes.* Somerville, MA: Candlewick Press, 2007.

Jeremy wishes he had stylish shoes like other boys in his school but his grandmother doesn't have enough money for the boots he *needs* and the shoes he *wants.* When Jeremy finally finds the shoes in a thrift shop, he's unconvinced that they're a size too small for him. In the end, Jeremy wrestles with a decision to give his new shoes to someone else who needs them and discovers that this act of kindness feels as good as getting new shoes.

Bunting, Eve. *Fly Away Home.* Boston: Houghton Mifflin Harcourt, 1993.

Although slightly dated, *Fly Away Home* still has its virtues. A little boy and his father live in an airport terminal in ways that were possible before September 11, but the embarrassment and humility that the family experiences is still relevant and worth using for a discussion about homelessness and what it must feel like to try to hide it, and reasons why someone might want to do that.

Coles, Robert. *The Story of Ruby Bridges.* New York: Scholastic Paperbacks, 2004.

The story of six-year-old Ruby Bridges is of one of courage, faith, and hope. When she enters first grade at an all-white school, Ruby is faced by an angry mob of white parents who do not want their children to go to school with her. Ruby's story can be discussed in the context of Jesus's commandment to love our neighbor, and how she was treated was not a Christian response. Encourage children to think about Ruby's story if everyone were following Jesus, and what that would have felt like for Ruby. Draw attention to Ruby's use of prayer, especially as she asks God to forgive the mob of grownups who shouted at her as she entered school each day.

Cooper, Ilene. *The Golden Rule.* New York: Abrams Books, 2007.

A grandfather explains to his grandson the meaning of the Golden Rule, and the universality of such a rule in other cultures and religions. The young boy imagines a world where everyone followed the rule, and his grandfather tells him, "It starts with you." This book expresses the common moral commitment in many religions in a helpful way while also being honest about the difficulty of adhering to such a rule. Have children ponder a world where everyone follows the Golden Rule, what it would look like, how they would feel, and then how we can stay hopeful when others don't follow it.

Dobrin, Arthur. *Love Your Neighbor: Stories of Values and Virtues.* New York: Scholastic, 1999.

A collection of stories about caring for others, this book is most appropriate for younger children who will love the furry characters who act out of kindness and love. Each story ends with a thought-provoking question to further the conversation, but teachers and children can extend learning further by imagining that they were the characters or by finding ways to share how they, too, have acted out of love and kindness.

Fox, Mem. *Wilfred Gordon McDonald Partridge.* La Jolla, CA, Kane/Miller Book Publishers, 1989.

A little boy, Wilfred Gordon McDonald Partridge, befriends a woman in a nearby nursing home because she also has four names. When he learns that Miss Nancy Alison Delacourt Cooper has lost her memory, he is determined to find it, collecting items from other residents that spark memories in his new friend. This is a useful story for discussing the importance of elders, and the unique friendship that both children and elders can offer. Encourage children to think creatively about who is a friend and what qualities are important in a friendship.

Goeminne, Siska. *No One Else Like You.* Louisville, KY: Westminster John Knox Press, 2016.

This book takes the reader through the many different kinds of people in the world, touching on not *only* physical differences, but the less visible differences still detectable by children like personality, temperament, and likes and dislikes. Children will like seeing parts of themselves honored in upbeat and honest words with attractive and playful illustrations.

Graham, Bob. *How to Heal a Broken Wing.* Somerville, MA: Candlewick Press, 2008.

A little boy, Will, is the only one in a crowd of adults who notices a bird with a broken wing. In this story, Will—with the help of his parents—tends to the bird with patience and determination until the bird can once again fly.

Grant, Jennifer. *Maybe God Is Like That Too*. Minneapolis, MN: Sparkhouse, 2017.

A little boy's curiosity about God leads him and his grandmother around the city to find God in places where they notice love, joy, and peace. This story encourages children—and adults—to find God in familiar acts of patience, kindness, and goodness.

Hall, Michael. *Red: A Crayon's Story*. New York: Greenwillow Books, 2015.

Following the story of a blue crayon that is mistaken as red, this encourages readers to be true to their inner selves, despite challenges and obstacles along the way. This book is helpful when discussing peer pressure, bullying, and gender identity. Invite children to think of times that someone wanted them to be red when they were feeling blue inside. How did they handle that? Who was helpful? What did they learn? Normalize the challenge of feeling different inside while also finding ways to accept ourselves as we are and surrounding ourselves with people who accept us.

Hardie, Jill. *The Sparkle Box: A Gift with the Power to Change Christmas*. Nashville, TN: Ideals Children's Books, 2012.

The Sparkle Box is a favorite at Christmas time and gives children a way to appreciate the celebration of Jesus's birth in a way that is more consistent with his life and teachings than many of our holiday customs may be. A heartwarming story about a little boy's interest in a sparkly box on the mantle and how he learns that its contents are the gift to Jesus: full of the kind and loving gestures for others in need. Encourage families to participate by filling their sparkle boxes with gifts for Jesus throughout the Christmas season.

Kilodavis, Cheryl. *My Princess Boy*. New York: Simon & Schuster, 2010.

Dyson is a little boy who likes pink, princesses, and all things pretty. A heartwarming story about a little boy who likes "girl things" that spends less time focusing on the ridicule and more on the unconditional love from his family who accepts him just as he is. This book is an excellent conversation piece about being different, the courage it sometimes takes, and the loving, Christian response to people who are different. Spend time talking about Dyson as a person, noticing that he appeared to be kind, loving, and a good friend—and that these are more important attributes than what someone is wearing or how they are playing.

Lamothe, Matt. *This is How We Do It.* San Francisco: Chronicle Books, 2017.

This story follows six children around the world, exploring the different ways each child eats, goes to school, dresses, learns, and plays. A great conversation piece for embracing differences and finding similarities among people that look and live differently but who are still made and loved by God.

Lloyd-Jones, Sally. *Baby Wren and the Great Gift.* Grand Rapids, MI: Zonderkidz.

Ideal for younger children, this story follows a baby wren that wonders why she doesn't have the gifts of other animals. As the story unfolds, the baby wren finds her own special gifts and ends with a feeling of gratitude of what she has and what she has to offer.

Lucado, Max. *The Oak Inside the Acorn.* Nashville, TN: Thomas Nelson, 2011.

The Oak Inside the Acorn is a story about the miraculous and special capacity that each of us has. The acorn wonders what will become of him: will he grow oranges like the orange tree, flowers like the rose bush? As he awaits his own purpose, his mother's words ring in his ears, "Just be the tree God made you to be." Take time to ponder Little Acorn's desire to grow oranges or rose blooms, and how God's plan for him was different, but just as important.

Ludwig, Trudy. *The Invisible Boy.* New York: Penguin Random House, 2013.

This is one of our favorite books and is a useful conversation piece about socially invisible people. The artwork lends itself to questions about how Brian is feeling, how easily others ignore him, and what small though loving actions make him visible to a new friend. Invite children to think how the characters are feeling in the story, including Brian, the children who ignore him, and his new friend.

Patel, Andrea. *On That Day*. Berkeley, CA: Tricycle Press, 2001.

Inspired by the events of September 11, *On That Day* offers a message of hope when confronted with hatred, violence, and destruction. Written in ways that are appropriate for young children, this book is a catalyst for conversation about how we feel when bad things happen, and then points us toward a more hopeful message of how much good there is in the world.

de la Peña, Matt. *Last Stop on Market Street*. New York: Penguin Random House, 2015.

This story addressed a child's questions and desires to have what others have and his grandmother's loving response that encourages him to see the beauty in their own routine and ritual of daily life. Invite children to talk about times when they've felt envious, normalizing this natural feeling; discuss and discover ways to tell ourselves that our own life is full of beautiful things, moments and people that make it different from the lives that others lead, but equally special.

de la Peña, Matt. *Love*. New York: G. P. Putnam's Sons, 2018.

Attractive pictures and loving words take the reader through the different places and ways in which love can be found. This story expands our idea of what love is, finding it in often overlooked places like a parent going off to work at dawn. The diversity of the illustrations can spark conversations about how love is found in all sorts of places, between all sorts of people.

Sanna, Francesca. *The Journey*. London: Flying Eye Books, 2016.

Ideal for children in grades 2 and up, *The Journey* is a tale of a family who must leave their home to escape war and turmoil. This story opens children's eyes to the reality of other children in war-torn parts of the world. For this topic and this book, in particular, it's important to pay attention to the children and families in your community and whether they are refugees or have family and/or friends who are living in places where their safety is a concern. If that is the case, make that part of your conversation and how war is affecting children in your own community.

Seuss, Dr. *Yertle the Turtle and Other Stories*. New York: Random House, 1958.

Children need to be reminded that things that are difficult, which include standing up for yourself or others, confront everyone. With this book, focus on how Mack and the other turtles were feeling, and what courageous action he took to help himself and others. It's also worth noting to children that Mack's actions were non-violent and not unkind, showing children that there are ways to respond to unkindness in ways that don't compromise our commitment to treat others the way we want to be treated.

Shannon, George. *One Family*. New York: Farrar, Straus and Giroux, 2015.

Through pictures, this book shows the many different ways a family can look, including size, age, and race. This book is ideal for younger grades and can lead into a conversation about who is in *their* family and how families are similar and different, but always includes people that love and take care of one another. A useful exercise would be to ask what a family *must* have and what it *can* have. For example, while families *can* have mothers, fathers, or siblings, not all do. What each family *must* have, though, is love.

Spinelli, Ellen. *Somebody Loves You, Mr. Hatch*. New York: Simon and Schuster Books, 1996.

The story of Mr. Hatch is about the power of love. When Mr. Hatch receives a valentine message "Somebody loves you," his life and his outlook begin to change. Through acts of love and kindness, Mr. Hatch makes new friends that continue to make him feel loved, even after he learns that the valentine was meant for someone else. This is a beautiful representation of how feeling loved can make us love ourselves and love others.

Stead, Philip C. *A Sick Day for Amos McGee*. New York: Macmillan Publishers, 2010.

This book presents a story about Amos, a man who visits friends in the zoo, but who falls ill one day and is not able to visit. The animals make the trip to Amos's house and take care of him while he recovers from a cold. This is a gentle and loving story about unique friendships that are based on caring for each other. Children can easily relate to the similarities between Amos's friendships and their own. Pose questions like, "What kind things do *you* do for your friends?"

Turner, Matthew P. *When God Made You*. Colorado Springs, CO: WaterBrook, 2017.

A singsong book about how God made us to be unique and special, this story follows a little girl as she encounters all of the things that God made about her. A celebration of the gifts of a child, from hair color to giggles, this book is an upbeat reminder that God made each of us different, but special and lovable.

Tutu, Desmond, and Abrams, Douglas C. *God's Dream*. Somerville, MA: Candlewick Press, 2008.

If God's dream came true, it might look a lot like *God's Dream*: people caring, sharing, and loving, doing our best to keep from hurting one another, but finding ways to reconcile and forgive when it inevitably happens. Children can easily identify with the scene of two children arguing; these interactions are normalized by saying that God doesn't ask us to be friends, but that we must care about one another. This is a helpful reminder that loving one another is important, even if sometimes challenging.

Vivas, Julie. *The Nativity*. Boston: Houghton Mifflin Harcourt, 2006.

With only Scripture as text, the drawings in this simple but powerful book portray the birth of Jesus in a way that resonates with all families who have experienced the birth of a new baby. Paired with the drawings, the Scripture is easier to comprehend and makes this important story feel more relatable not only to children—but to everyone.

Williams, Laura E. *The Can Man*. New York: Lee & Low Books, 2017.

This is a heart-warming story about a young boy and his family's insistence on dignifying a former neighbor turned homeless who is "down on his luck." Tim is anxious to buy a new skateboard with the money he's earned, but—at the last minute—finds a better use for his earnings that tends to the need of this former neighbor, "The Can Man." Tim's story is a testament that giving can be better than receiving, and that tending to the needs of others—even if not the easiest thing to do—is always the right thing to do.

Williams, Vera B. *A Chair for My Mother*. New York: Greenwillow Books, 2007.

A book about love and tenderness, this story is about one family's adversity that brings them together to tend to their grandmother who needs a chair to rest. Themes of gratitude, hard work, and optimism can all be discussed with this book about a family's love for one another.

Witek, Jo. *In My Heart: A Book of Feelings*. New York: Abrams Books, 2014.

Asked to answer, "How does your heart feel?" this book honors the many feelings that we have, including shyness, sadness, excitement, and anger. This book helps normalize the many feelings that children have that don't feel good but are all part of being human. This book can spark conversations about what it looks like when we have these feelings, how we manage these feelings in ways that don't hurt others, or ourselves, and ways that we can make ourselves feel better.

Woodson, Jacqueline. *Each Kindness*. New York: Nancy Paulsen Books, 2012.

Maya is a new girl who is ignored and teased by her classmates. When she moves, one child is left with regret and a willingness to change, but with no opportunity to do so. A story about being kind to others and the effects our actions—whether positive or negative—can have on others is a theme that resonates with readers of all ages.

Woodson, Jacqueline. *The Other Side*. New York: G. P. Putnam's Sons, 2001.

When two little girls' mothers—one black, one white—tell them not to cross to the other side of the fence, the girls find a way to connect by sitting together *on* the fence. A sweet story about two little girls who find a way around segregation to start a new friendship, *The Other Side* is a lesson in doing what's right, even if you're surrounded by people encouraging you to do otherwise.

Yamada, Kobi. *What Do You Do With a Problem?* Seattle, WA: Compendium, Inc., 2016.

A story about facing our fears and what can happen when we do, this book can spark conversation about our anxieties and what opportunities might lie inside them. For anyone who has ever had a problem, this story will encourage us to be courageous and brave to face our fears.

Chapter Books

Parents of children in the upper grades regularly ask for book suggestions to help their children cope with anxiety, bullying, or to help develop empathy. Consider doing a book club for children in these grades, giving everyone the opportunity to read at home and using Sunday mornings as a time to discuss topics and themes that relate to courage, friendship, loving ourselves and our neighbors.

Khan, Hena. *Amina's Voice*. New York: Simon and Schuster, 2017.

This is in some ways a standard adolescent tale of having courage, fitting in, making hard choices, and showing understanding to friends and peers. But all these issues are further complicated when Amina's mosque is set on fire in a hate crime. This book thus can help readers talk through many of the common challenges of late childhood or adolescence, while also introducing concepts of religious difference, tolerance, and acceptance.

Lin, Grace. *Where the Mountain Meets the Moon.* New York: Little, Brown Books for Young Readers, 2009.

Where the Mountain Meets the Moon is a long book, so is only suitable for older groups of children who might be especially interested in reading. It is a whimsical tale of fantasy and adventure that follows the adventures of a little girl named Minli, who is trying to help her poor family. Along the way she shows great kindness to strangers and thoughtfulness, and in the story's climactic scenes lives out lovely lessons of selflessness and thanksgiving. It's a beautiful book about cherishing what matters, and about sharing what matters most with others.

Palacio, R. J. *Wonder.* New York: Penguin Random House, 2012.

The story of ten-year-old Auggie Pullman who has a facial deformity, *Wonder* is written from multiple characters' perspectives, leaving the reader only a few pages to make judgments about a character's actions and reactions before learning that people can be much more complicated than they appear. Auggie's first year in a mainstream school is full of ups and downs, but all revolving around his differences, how people react, and his family's unconditional and unwavering love for him.

Rowling, J. K. *Harry Potter and the Sorcerer's Stone.* New York: Scholastic, 1998.

It's well known that J. K. Rowling self-consciously modeled her popular Harry Potter series of novels upon Christian themes, but the first in the series is especially appropriate for this age group. Issues of loyalty, friendship, goodness, judgment, and most of all the power of love, resonate throughout the text and will provide lots of opportunity for discussion.

Woodson, Jacqueline. *Feathers.* New York: Putnam, 2007.

Dealing with issues of hope, faith, race, religion, disability, difference, and kindness toward others, this book provides endless opportunities for discussion. The religious conclusions and confusions of some characters in the book, though they may not be ones you will want to endorse, can still provide a useful starting point for older children to discuss their own faith lives and will help to normalize the questioning and uncertainty that are part of any honest faith.